More Space.
More Time.
More Joy!

ORGANIZING
YOUR BEST LIFE

LISA DOOLEY

*Pat & Nancy~
Here's to creating
your best life!*

*Much joy!
Lisa*

More Space. More Time. More Joy!: Organizing Your Best Life, Published July, 2019

Cover Design: Howard Johnson
Interior Design and Layout: Howard Johnson
Editorial and Proofreading: Eden Rivers Editorial Services; Karen Grennan
Photo Credits: Maryellen Jones, MJ Design Studio

 **SDP Publishing**

Published by SDP Publishing, an imprint of SDP Publishing Solutions, LLC.

For more information about this book contact Lisa Akoury-Ross at SDP Publishing by e-mail at info@SDPPublishing.com.

SDP Publishing
Permissions Department
PO Box 26
East Bridgewater, MA 02333
or e-mail your request to info@SDPPublishing.com

ISBN-13 (print): 978-1-7327933-8-5
ISBN-13 (ebook): 978-1-7327933-9-2

Library of Congress Control Number: 2019941784

DEDICATION

I grew up in the most organized home you could imagine. My mother could have taught Hannibal a thing or two about getting those elephants across the Alps in a quicker, more efficient fashion. On a limited budget, my mother worked day and night to ensure that her home looked perfect and we looked perfect. My dad, the most obliging person you could ever meet, fell right into line, perfecting the phrase, "Yes, Mary," early on.

Clearly, I inherited many of my mother's organizing skills and some of her "need" for perfection. And of all the great memories I have of home-cooked meals, a sparkling clean house, hand sewn matching outfits complete with hats and gloves, one thing is missing. *Joy.* My mother worked tirelessly because she loved us and wanted us to have "the best" of everything. For her, organization *was* the goal; she wanted everything to be in its place. Because of this, she rarely rested and enjoyed herself or life during those busy years. In her later years, she traveled and connected more and slowed down enough to step fully into her life. I think she would have agreed, in the end, that all that perfection wasn't really the best goal. *More joy* is the most important goal of all.

This book is dedicated to my mom, and my wish for all of you is *more space, more time,* and *more joy.*

TABLE OF CONTENTS

INTRODUCTION

"Things don't change; we change."

—from *Walden*, by Henry David Thoreau

⤬

I've always loved this Thoreau quote. Surprisingly, it took me a long time in my own organizing practice (longer than I'd like to admit) to understand that change, real change, was internal. I *knew* I could create systems and solutions for clients to help them get organized. I could coach clients on time "management," paperwork management, filing systems, and space organization to provide transferable skills to make their lives both at work and home more organized and less stressful. I could be the "tool in their toolbox" to solve problems, find solutions, and make real and lasting change. I couldn't organize them because organizing is an intuitive process—but more on that later. As hard as I tried and as diligently as we worked together, real change didn't come until clients started to see their organizing challenges and themselves differently.

Organizing isn't about boxes and bins. It isn't about matching folders and overly complicated filing systems. Organizing isn't alphabetizing your spice rack and color coding your sock drawer. If you have time to do those things, STOP. Call a friend, go for a walk, read a book, find your passion in work or community and *go live your life.* In this manic, overscheduled, digitally connected world, we continually add layers of complexity onto our lives that frankly, we really don't need. Sure, I love The Container Store and for an organizer, that catalog is like candy. But that's *not* real life.

Real life and true organizing is about finding your stuff when you need it. When I can find my stuff when I need it, I have time to do the things I really want to do and spend time with those I love. That's it. You don't need a complicated system to be organized. You need to see the value of being organized and know that you deserve to live your best life. We are unable to live our best life when we are surrounded by clutter and things that are holding us back and holding us down. Being organized helps us find more space, more time, and most importantly, more joy in our lives.

Over years of working with clients, I learned that while every organizing challenge is inherently unique in its own way, there are also striking similarities. At the root of disorganization is a misuse of space and time. Disorganization tends to take hold during and after a transition—a new baby, a move, new job, illness, or death of a loved one. These transitions can be either positive or negative, but they always involve change. Systems that once worked fall apart and disorganization takes hold. It's during this time that stress starts to build around the disorganization and we may become overwhelmed. I've worked with clients who've lived with this level of stress and disorganization for years. The compound effect of this is frustration and often low-grade unhappiness and dissatisfaction with life. What I strive for in each client relationship is to help clients rewrite the stories of their lives—from frustrated, stressed, and unable to enjoy their space and their lives to seeing their homes and offices as places of calm, rejuvenation, and productivity.

In each situation, I need to understand the client's goal and how they want to live differently. More importantly, I need to understand a client's why—why they want to get organized. The turning point in my organizing practice was reading *Start with Why* by Simon Sinek. If you have not read this book, read it now—after you finish this book of course. The crux of Sinek's argument is that *why* we do something is much more valuable and has much greater impact than *how* we do something. I then understood that getting clients to resonate with their why and then building an organizational action plan around that made the process that much easier. Internalizing the why—the change we are creating—sets the change into motion and generates its strength and staying power.

This book is a guide to starting the process of change that will allow you to intentionally create your best life through organization. Organization is not the end goal; joy and living your best life is the goal. Organization is a means to getting to that end. Start with the vision of what you want your life and space to be: light, open, full of possibility and potential. Is that different from how you see your life right now? That's okay. We're in this together so let's get started....

Part I

More Space

Space is finite. And yet we pretend and convince ourselves that somehow, our already overcrowded space can hold *just a little bit* more.... In science, we know that nature abhors a vacuum. Have space; will fill it. And what will you fill your space with? More possessions? More tchotchkes, more trinkets, more stuff?

What we bring into our lives is reflective of how we value ourselves. Let's talk about finding more space for what's really important to you....

1

How Do I Get Started?

"The journey of 1,000 miles begins with a first step...."

—Lao Tzu

As a professional organizer and coach, I help my clients find more space, more time, and *more joy* in their lives. It's not uncommon for clients to come to me after years of living with disorganization, which resulted in stress and frustration. Working together, I coach clients so that they can transform their lives from being stressed, overwhelmed, and unhappy to living a fuller, more present and intentional life. Organizing isn't boxes or bins. It's not fancy systems or products. It's finding your stuff when you need it so you can go and live your best life.

Have you ever watched TV shows like *Hoarders* and thought that's what disorganization is? Well, it isn't—that's filth and hoarding. Yes, there are some people who do actually live like that but that is a *very* small percentage. The American Psychiatric Association has classified hoarding as a mental illness and someone with a true hoarding disorder often has other emotional challenges as well. Situations shown on those shows have developed over years and years and will take almost as long to rectify. And no, you can't just "throw out the junk" and problem solved. *Why* we accumulate and hold onto things is really at the heart of the issue. For someone with hoarding tendencies and behaviors, eliminating a certain item can cause real stress and anxiety and is immediately replaced by another *thing*. Do you feel that even though you may be living with clutter and disorganization, at least you're not *that bad*? Getting organized is a process, not an event. Are you ready to take the first step?

For many clients, one day something just clicks—call it an "AHA moment"—and the client decides they cannot live like this for another instant. For each client, that pivotal moment or event is different. Unfortunately, this is rarely a positive event. Generally, it's an unhappy experience or even an unkind remark about their cluttered space that really hits home. Perhaps they are unable or unwilling to host a party or have family and friends over because they are embarrassed or unhappy with the way the home looks. Sometimes a well-meaning friend or family member makes a remark about "cleaning up" or offering to help "get rid of the junk." Most of the time, clients are very aware that there's a problem with clutter and disorganization—that's the difference between true hoarding and disorganization. For most clients, they're just immobilized by an inability to move forward and make change. There's an old saying that the definition of insanity is doing the same thing over and over and expecting a different outcome. For many clients, they feel "stuck" in a negative pattern. It isn't until clients experience that level of frustration and stress that they decide to do something differently.

Regardless if your home is 1,400 or 3,400 or 5,400 square feet, many clients believe they need more space for stuff. According to the U.S. self storage industry, as of December 2018, one in nine Americans had a storage unit[1]—what the heck are we putting in there? We live in an accumulation culture where buying and shopping are recreation. We buy knickknacks and tchotchkes and trinkets and *stuff* because we have the discretionary income to do so and idle time to fill. Unlike previous generations, we have more time and more money and we don't believe in saving for a rainy day or the future like our parents did. Instead, we buy. The marketing machine tells us we need to purchase more, and newer, and fancier versions of stuff we already own and we fill our houses and offices to the rafters with our stuff. And *then* we fill our storage units.

At some point, we started to believe that we could buy happiness—that by purchasing just the right shoes/car/electronics/ TV, *then* we'd be happy. In effect, we place our faith in external things to make us happy. The result of this consumer-driven mentality is that we have so much stuff we really don't know what to do with. Buying and keeping and buying some more has become recreation for us. We buy because we're sad; we buy because we're grieving; we buy because we think it will make us happy. Regardless of whether we can truly afford the things we buy, the true psychological price we are paying for all this stuff is much higher than we believe. The temporary high we get from a new purchase is quickly replaced by boredom, buyer's remorse, and the reality that this thing cannot bring us happiness. Happiness is created internally; it cannot be purchased. Another buying trap many people fall into is the "it was free/discounted/on sale/such a good deal" concept. I love a bargain as much as the next person, but just because something was a "good deal" doesn't mean you need to buy five or ten of it. I cannot count how many times I've watched a client throw out food, health and beauty products, medication, and other items because they are expired and/or unusable. So that "great deal" of purchasing in bulk was really just a waste of money in the end.

Organizing Tip

Unless you have an *immediate upcoming* need for multiples of the same item, resist the lure! The BOGO and discount sales are really an attempt to drive up consumption and sales volume.

So how did we go from a nation of producers and manufacturers to a nation of consumers? How did this happen?

Have you ever looked around your space—either at home or work—and thought "where the heck did all this stuff come from?" This is especially true for couples who have been together for a few years and have settled into a home. The tricky part is that stuff enters our space in a multitude of ways and the volume has a way of sneaking up on us. As adults, we buy the necessities we need in our homes like the bedroom set you purchased when you got married. And the pots and pans. And the recliner, couch, and of course the new TV for when you're sitting on the couch. This is all the stuff you've purchased together that's part of your "relationship life." Don't even get me started on sheet sets and towels—these seem to proliferate more than anything.... And, quite likely, you each brought stuff—often duplicate stuff—to your relationship and your home. And if you had space to store all this duplicate stuff, you just kept it and figured you'd make the decisions later.

In addition to all the stuff you've purchased yourself, there's the stuff you've been "gifted." Maybe you received it as a wedding gift and that lovely crystal or china is still sitting in the box, unused, unopened, in the basement, moved three times in ten years. Or you've inherited items from a family member who was sure you would LOVE this item. (Be wary of loved ones emptying their space by filling yours!)

The buck needs to stop here. If you are going to make real change in how you live your life and how you inhabit your space, this is the starting point. Think of yourself as a gate-keeper to organization. As the amazing organizer and author Peter Walsh so aptly said, "Nothing enters your space without your permission."[2] You must decide what comes in and what must go and yes, you need to get your family, housemates, and office mates on board.

Nothing comes into your home or office without your permission so that's really the critical point. "Something in, something out" is a great rule for managing volume in your home or office. Yes, yes, I do know what it's like to live with family members and office mates who bring stuff into our space every day. But you are the gatekeeper. Be the change and the example for how the space should be. It's a great idea to give each person a designated space for their "special stuff" (we all need it). Maybe it's space to display art or mementos or sports trophies or your beloved spoon collection. It doesn't matter what it is; what matters is that *we respect our stuff and our space.* We are not respecting our possessions and our space when everything is a cluttered jumble. If an item is important, display it and give it the respect it deserves or store it in a designated space. We all have stuff we consider important. An entire room dedicated to old band equipment your partner hasn't touched in twenty years is something to be negotiated.

Space is a limited thing and volume—which is often really the biggest organizing challenge—cannot exceed your space. Too much volume in too small of a space equals clutter and chaos. The first step in using the concept of "something in, something out" is to *really* understand what you already have.

For some of us, when we can't find what we are looking for, we purchase a second. Or a third. The result is that we have a multitude of the same item. So gather all the soccer cleats, hammers, black sweaters, phone chargers, etc.—whatever item you are organizing—and decide on how many of that item you really need to keep. Is three black sweaters the right number? Great, donate the rest. So that you can see and find them when you need them, decide where they should all be kept. Is it best to hang them in the master closet? Great, hang them up. Is the armoire in the guest room a better choice due to space constraints? Okay, fold them up and store them in the other room.

If you buy another black sweater, one of the "old" sweaters has to go. Something in, something out. This rule is especially important to remember and apply when you are shopping. Another black sweater might look like a great deal but remember, when you get home, one black sweater must go.

By doing this, you are limiting volume so that it does not exceed your space. If you force yourself to think and purchase by this organizing rule, you limit the things that enter the home and you save money, time, and space.

If you allow something into your already overcrowded space, where the heck are you going to put it? Space is finite so you have to decide what is truly worthy of entering your space. To reach your goal of living and intentional life through organization you must be selective on what enters your space. Let go of your old ideas about what being organized means. This is an opportunity to change course and rewrite the story of your life. The behaviors and choices you've made in the past aren't working now and this is the time to do different for a different result. Lew Platt, former CEO of Hewlett Packard, put it this way: "Whatever made you successful in the past won't in the future." Once you're *intentional* about what enters your space—home or office—you're on the path to organization.

Organizing Tip

Controlling what comes in and out of our space is one of the keys to staying organized and not allowing clutter to build. Yes, it's hard to manage other people's things but creating and applying this rule to everyone is key. "Something in, something out" manages volume and money.

2

How Do I Find More Space?

"The things you own end up owning you."

—Tyler Durden, *Fight Club*

he consumer mentality is everywhere. Buy, buy, buy and then you'll be happy. Happiness is just a "click of the cart" away. In this manic, consumer-driven environment, we spend more time consuming than we do living. We are no longer making intentional decisions and choices. We are allowing others to make our choices for us because we seem unwilling and unable to resist the allure of buying and spending. And the result is all this *stuff* in our lives.

In addition to all the stuff we purchase ourselves, the hidden space suckers are those things that come from others. Let's talk about how to manage the stuff from others. As humans, we are really good at creating "use scenarios" for most any item. Ben Franklin is credited as saying, "The man who is good at making excuses is seldom good at anything else." Yet still, we persist. *When we get a bigger house, we'll be able to use this extra bedroom set. Who doesn't need a second, third (or fourth!) couch in the basement? It seems like such a waste to let go of the rocking chair—I'll hold onto it until I redo my office and then I'll move it in there.* And the list goes on. …

You inherited Grandma's china set and the furniture from your childhood bedroom: How will you use it now? Ask this question before anything enters your space. What is the purpose or use for this item? Where do I store the crystal glassware I received as a wedding gift that still sits in the original box that I've moved three times and never opened? Am I ever going to use this crystal? Or this bread maker, pasta maker, smoothie machine—all those kitchen gadgets and electronics that sit unused and unneeded, taking up valuable space. The cribs, high chairs, strollers, walkers, etc. that you are tempted to save for "down the road" will likely be unsafe and unusable in a fairly short period of time. Donate and pass those items on immediately.

Some decisions will be easier and more clear-cut. And sometimes the answer to the question of "What is the purpose of this item?" will be, "I don't know." And that's okay. Sit with the question and revisit it in a few days. Once you've determined that the item in question doesn't have a purpose in your space, move it along. Anything we own comes with a cost beyond its initial purchase cost. After you buy the item, you then have to maintain, repair, and store it. Even items that have been passed on to you or have been received as a gift have a cost in maintenance and storage. If you own an abundance of items, they become a burden if the items are unneeded and unused.

Eliminating the items and their upkeep gains you time and money—limited and valuable commodities. If I didn't have to spend time repairing my stuff, could I spend more time with family and friends and doing the things I love? Instead of buying stuff, can I use my money for travel and adventure? By eliminating items that are unused and unneeded, you open up both physical and psychological space—thereby gaining more space in your home and in your life.

In working with clients over the years, I've recognized that one of the greatest challenges that clients face in making change and getting organized is fear. Fear of making a mistake, fear of someone else finding out about their stuff and their purchases, fear of being judged, fear of not being loved and not being "enough." So you insulate yourself against this fear by surrounding yourself with your stuff. Do you want things to be different? Do you want to live a different life? As American physician and psychotherapist Carl Whittaker says, "Success is letting go of fear."

Keep in your space the things that you need and the things that you love—that's it. *I need my coffeemaker and I love my glass end tables.* Keep them. *I need dishes and pots and pans and looking at my plate collection brings me joy.* Keep it. *I need my TV and I love watching movies on my DVD player.* Enjoy them. If something doesn't serve a purpose in your life and it doesn't bring you joy, then let it go.

One of the most common reasons that our homes become filled with clutter is that we feel "bad" and guilty about letting our things go. You purchased something; you don't love it or need it, and yet you can't decide to get rid of it. "I paid good money for that," is a common refrain with my clients. So you become unwilling to let things go out of fear of loss: loss of money, loss of use, and loss of pride. You are ashamed that you made a bad purchasing choice so you punish yourself by sticking it in a closet, in the basement, up in the attic, taking up your valuable space. This is a scarcity mentality driven by a belief that when we really need something in the future, it won't be there.

Not only is this unused and unneeded item taking up physical space, it's taking up psychic space in your head. Be kind and forgiving to yourself. In his wonderful book, *Authentic Success*, Robert Holden writes, "Shame holds you back and forgiveness moves you forward." You made a "mistake"—let it go and get rid of the physical and emotional baggage so you can create the organized life you want to live. In upcoming chapters, I'll talk about the myriad of ways to recoup some of the money you spend on your stuff and do good at the same time.

Finding more space and more time are the two most common challenges for many of us. *How do I find space in my home and office for the things I really need and love? How do I open psychic space in my head and quiet all the noise?* Finding and creating more time is another common organizing goal for my clients. *So how do I find space and time in my life?* You will find more space, more time, and more joy by letting go of the stuff that's holding you down and holding you back.

We find joy when we are truly in the moment and doing something we enjoy. In a space overcrowded with unneeded and unused items, we cannot find joy. If we are spending our time and money buying, fixing, maintaining and trying to find our stuff, we lose time that could be better spent doing something we love. In a 2017 study, it was estimated that Americans spend 2.5 days a YEAR trying to find something—a book, the phone charger, an insurance policy, the car keys. In addition to lost time, the cost for replacing these items is valued at $27 billion a year.[3] If

Organizing Tip

"No thank you." is a complete sentence. Use it wisely to keep unwanted and unneeded items out of your space.

we keep only those things that serve us and bring us joy in an organized way, we won't waste time looking for things. What could you do with another two and a half days a year? And what do you want to spend your time and money on? An adventure? Travel? Time with family and friends? Your answer indicates what's important to you.

Would you be surprised to learn that being organized can also be good for the environment and your wallet? When we're disorganized, we're not making good choices with our time and resources. If we are not in control of our time, we pay late fees, interest fees, and other penalties. We repurchase items because we are not aware of what we already have in our pantry, closet, or storage unit. This leads into the issues of volume and overspending. Rampant consumerism is at odds with living an intentional, mindful life.

There are some simple, mindful steps that you can take to save money and resources as well as reduce your footprint on our planet: Reduce, Reuse, and Recycle. Reducing the volume that enters your space is the first important step. There are things in life you cannot control but what comes into your space *is* something you can control. Nothing comes into your space without your permission. Reducing the volume of what enters is a starting point. You will have less stuff to deal with and less to organize now and in the future. If it's your goal to live an intentional and organized life, you must become the gate-keeper to your space. I know that this is a challenge for families and organizations; no one likes to be the meanie or the bad guy. You must state clearly for family members and co-workers what your goals and intentions are; do not be ambiguous or vague. Understand that if this is a change—especially if it is a radical change in how things have been in the past—know that there will be some resistance and growing pains.

Once you have a handle on what is coming into the space, focus on how to best utilize what you already have instead of buying new stuff. Can you reuse an item in a different space or for another purpose for greater effectiveness? Can a bookshelf or table originally in a bedroom be reused in the playroom or entryway? Baskets and bins that once housed toys in the kids' bedroom? Reuse them in the craft room for yarns and other craft supplies.

Recycling has the connotation of keeping things out of the trash, and yes, that's one way to look at it. I encourage

Organizing Tip

Organizing doesn't require elaborate systems and products. A system can often be created with existing items. When starting an organizing project, resist the urge to go out and purchase boxes and bins or fancy organizing systems. First reuse what you already have and "shop at home" to find organizing solutions without buying new products and spending money.

clients to be mindful about recycling but not dogmatic. I have worked with clients to tweak recycling systems that were just plain ineffective. You don't need an elaborate system for most home-based recycling. Do not create obstacles to achieving your goal, which is eliminating more of what goes into our landfills. Avoid creating another problem with your process. Receptacles that are undersized or ineffective, bins set up in inconvenient areas, processes that are multi-stepped and overly complicated are time wasters and self-defeating.

When it comes to items in your home, recycling has an additional purpose. Purging what you don't use and don't need and recycle—pass on anything still in good, usable condition. You can find a list of resources at the back of the book to donate just about anything. For most of us, when we can't find what we are looking for, we purchase another, and then another. Our consumerism feeds the belief that if one is good, two is better so the volume builds. So gather all the soccer cleats, hammers, black sweaters, phone chargers, etc.—whatever item/category you are organizing—and decide on how many you *really* need to keep.

Don't limit the idea of recycling to what you can give away through donation. If you resell an item through online yard sales, eBay, and other sources, you also cut down on the manufacturing of new items that contributes to the health of our planet. The Reduce, Reuse, and Recycle model saves money, time, and resources for you and others.

Clearing out the clutter and the noise in our lives gives us back lost space and time. Space, time, and money are finite. Let go of the stuff that's cluttering up your life so you can find more space, more time, and more joy.

3

What Is Transitional Space?

"Make it easy to do right and hard to go wrong."
—Gretchen Rubin, "Here's My Habits Manifesto.
What's Yours?"

Have you ever heard the term "launching/landing pad"? (This isn't your private helicopter pad but that would be very cool.) In organizer-speak, this refers to the space where you "launch" into your day and "land" back into when you return. In a nutshell, it's the transitional space between being outside and being inside. The goal of the launching/landing pad is to get you in and out with less stress and in less time. When this space contains the items you need every day when you enter and exit, you don't have to continually search your entire home or office for the things you need. Think purse, backpack, gym bag, everyday coats, and of course, keys. If you can find your keys, grab your work bag, and get out the door in the morning without a crisis, you start your day with a win. No one wants to start the day with a meltdown over a missing backpack or misplaced car keys. Give yourself the first victory of the day by getting everyone out the door on a good note.

While a traditional mudroom space or entryway are the easiest examples, any transitional space makes your entire home or office function more efficiently. If this launching/landing pad doesn't already exist in a traditional sense, create it. When I work with clients designing a launching/landing pad, this is always a highly customized solution and needs to be intuitive to how the users and the space functions. If you are a family with young children, customize for their use now so that everyone can access and utilize the space. At the same time, remember that in a couple of years, they will be taller and their bags and backpacks will be *much* bigger. Clients often spend a lot of money on fancy cubby systems that work great for preschoolers and are Pinterest-worthy. But trust me when I tell

Organizing Tip

Plan for today and tomorrow when choosing organizing systems and solutions. You don't need to spend a lot of money "outfitting" your transitional space, but you do need to create an effective plan. Form follows function—not the other way around.

you that a middle schooler's backpack will not fit in those cute little cubbies. Instead, they'll end up on the floor along with their coats that don't fit on those cute little hooks inside those narrow cubbies.

In a commercial or business space, there is often an entryway or hallway leading into the office. Decide what furniture and storage works best. Is there an entryway closet? Great. Stock it with solid wooden hangers for coats—not flimsy wire or plastic versions. Simple additions like an umbrella stand make a huge impact, especially on visitors. Other great additions? A small table and a trash can. Have a spot for your visitors and employees to put their things down and hang up coats. A trash can allows them to throw out anything they've carried in from outside. Organization isn't about fancy boxes and bins and complicated systems. Reportedly Einstein said, "Everything should be made as simple as possible, but not simpler." Don't overthink it; don't overcomplicate it.

To create your own landing pad figure out what works best for you and your space. Ask, "What is the exit/entrance that I use most often?" Do you exit the house into the garage? If so, create your transitional space by the door inside the garage or at the door leading to it. I've helped a number of clients create really effective spaces within the garage or at its entrance. What's great about using this area is that sometimes there's more space available and you aren't as constricted by the need to create a certain "look." Your company isn't seeing that space so you don't have to be as concerned about how it looks. The space needs to function well and serve your needs.

The Launching/Landing Pad that Changed Everything

One of my favorite clients, S., is an active, engaged mom, wife, and a truly wonderful person. Parenting two young daughters, volunteering, teaching religious ed, and being an amazing partner to her husband, she had a lot going on. When we started working together, one of her biggest challenges was getting everyone in and out of the house in a less stressful way. They had done a great renovation a couple of years prior and had created some great cubbies and storage space in the expanded kitchen next to the kitchen door. Intended to be a resource for daily items, it wasn't working ideally, because that wasn't their true transitional space. Instead the family exited and entered through the garage; so we needed to focus on creating the launching/landing pad at that entrance.

Inside the garage, we divided the big space into zones using the "kindergarten method." Auto supplies, gardening, toys and bikes, home repair items, and overflow pantry items got their own space. First we purged the unneeded and unused including leftover renovation supplies, which she donated to Habitat for Humanity. We used existing wire racking set up on the perimeter to store items up and off the garage floor—a major stumbling block to easy transitions. From an office supply company, we purchased large, resin cabinets for pantry supplies. In a space like a garage or basement that can get dusty, closed storage

(continued)

like this is ideal. With the rest of the garage items, we containerized as much as possible into bins and crates, which made the new system much easier to navigate. Now we could focus on the launching/landing pad.

At the entrance to the house, we stationed a repurposed large, metal table for items going in and out of the house. This eliminated too many items in the kitchen and stuff taking up space on the countertop. This also became the spot for storing items to go in and out of the cars: sports bags, dance costumes, anything moving in and out. Above and around the door, we added lots and lots of hooks for hanging dog leashes, coats, umbrellas and anything else we could hang up. (Anytime you can hang something up, you eliminate clutter on horizontal surfaces.)

Using the newly designed space took some trial and error and some "training" for the rest of the family. Moving everything to the perimeter of the garage opened up the middle so parking two cars was easy and there was a system and routine for entering and exiting the space.

And S.? We had coffee recently and I'm thrilled to say she's as lovely as ever!

The key is to use the entrance that works best for your situation. The key to creating usable transitional space is not only *where* it is located but *how* you use it. Choose appropriate storage to section off an area at the door for your transitional space. Use this space to corral those items you will be taking with you as you exit. The most needed items are often keys, purses, gym/work bags, backpacks, coats, and shoes. When you re-enter the space, use the storage (hooks, hangers, bins) to house the items here.

The goal of effective transitional space is to not carry these items further into the home/office. If we leave our "everyday" items in the launching/landing pad, you won't need to regather them again the next time you leave. Figure out what belongs there and make sure it stays there and does not migrate into the rest of the home or office where it is likely to get misplaced.

"To do two things at once is to do neither," noted the Latin writer Publilius Syrus. To make your transitional space work for you, be intentional and thoughtful when you enter. Stop acting on autopilot and focus on what you're really doing.

Most of us are familiar with the safety phrase "stop, drop, and roll" as it relates to fire safety. The idea behind this safety phrase is that we don't continue a moment longer when we sense danger. We stop, drop to the ground, and roll out the fire. So, think about it this way. When creating your launching/landing pad, and its organizing systems, think about your stop, drop, and roll. By first stopping in your transitional space, you consciously keep from bringing anything that doesn't belong further into your other spaces. By doing this, it forces you to focus on your next steps.

When you drop, you keep the appropriate items housed in that

Organizing Tip

When you enter your space, stop and think about what you need to do first. Drop your items in the transitional space (which includes hanging up what needs to be hung up) and roll into your next activity or space.

space. Dropping doesn't mean dropping everything on the floor or the horizontal spaces. We make this part of the process easier by having the right storage—hooks, hangers, baskets, bins—whatever is best. Did you hang up your coat and work bag? Are the keys and backpack in their right spot? Take the time to hang up or put away items as appropriate. Using the storage options you've created makes this process accessible and you are using the space to its best advantage. When you've done your appropriate drop, everything in this space that should stay is stored. Now it's readily available for the next exit. Get ready to roll into the next part of your day with intention, and without dragging everything into the rest of the space.

Most of us pass through our transitional space so many times a day that we don't focus on that space or how it can work best for us. When used appropriately, it can be a really useful and critical part of your home and office. Be intentional about what goes in that space. Being organized takes intention and mindfulness. When you stop, drop, and roll in your launching/landing pad, you are focused on making that space work for you.

4

KISS: Keep It Seriously Simple

"Every good plan must be a servant, not a master."

—Robert Holden, *Authentic Success*

instein has been credited for saying, "The significant problems we face cannot be solved at the same level of thinking we were at when we created them." Put more simply—start thinking differently to address your organizing challenges. Think simple, effective solutions and systems that are easy to maintain. The organizing challenges in each home and office are unique based on the layout, organizational needs, and items in the space. Now that you've chosen your transitional space, you'll need to customize it.

So, what's the best storage solution in that space: hooks or hangers? Use the KISS method—Keep It Seriously Simple—to decide on the best option. I use this expression in its different iterations with clients often so that we don't over-complicate a solution and end up creating a different challenge down the road. In transitional space, hooks are the easiest solution. Everyone, including young children, can hang something up. Hooks are ideal for coats, bags, backpacks—just about anything with a strap or loop.

Using a hook requires the least amount of time and effort and is a nonnegotiable way to keep your transitional space clear and uncluttered. Another plus of using hooks—either single hooks, known as butler hooks, or a rack with multiple hooks—is that it is a very cost-effective solution. You don't need anything more than wall space and a screwdriver to install. If you have a lot of vertical wall space, you can install two racks of hooks—one higher and one lower—and double your storage. This is not rocket science. This is using the space that's available to maximize your storage and organizational solutions for the easiest maintenance and at the lowest cost.

Hangers also have a use in transitional space. In an office setting, a closet with hangers is a more professional option for business attire. For the home, a hall closet with quality hangers is ideal for guests and less frequently used coats. If you are creating a launching/landing pad out of a non-traditional space, you will need to limit the use of hangers. Hangers and the space for them take up extra storage. It also takes more time to use a hanger. Yes, realistically it takes about *30 seconds longer* to use a hanger versus a hook. But as

Organizing Tip

Invest in good quality hangers for your transitional space and other closets. Choose solid wood hangers for coats and flocked or acrylic/plastic hangers for a wardrobe. In the words of the immortal Joan Crawford: "No more wire hangers!" Wire hangers work for dress shirts and blouses and not much else. More to come on that in a later section....

we are rushing in and out and you need to decide between hooks and hangers, that 30 seconds can mean the difference between that item being hung up or hitting the floor.

Once you've selected the spot for your launching/landing pad and determined how you want to use it, think about ease of use. Each space is unique, but ideally you will have both open and closed storage in the space. An example of open storage is a coat rack/coat hooks, and a large basket on the floor for hats, winter items, or sports equipment. Open storage is best used for "grab and go" items and anything we need to see often and access easily.

If possible, try to incorporate closed storage as well. In transitional space, cabinets or benches with lids are ideal. This is particularly useful for storing items we need—think boots, bug spray, and sunscreen—but don't necessarily need to access on a daily basis. Want to guess how many mudrooms and closets I've seen overflowing with snow boots *in June*? Lots. It's important to clear out what you don't need on a daily basis and save that critical and useful space. Clients often choose closed storage because it looks neater, but beware of the buildup of non-essential items. Because the stuff is behind closed doors, it's particularly good for items that aren't easily containerized or are especially bulky or messy. Closets and cabinets are more likely to be found in office spaces because they are part of the design process. You can also add closed storage to most transitional spaces. Closed benches, armoires, and cubby systems are great additions to your launching/landing pad and make tidying up that space easier.

Remember reduce, reuse, and recycle? This is another good opportunity to "shop at home" so think about repurposing storage from another part of the home. Bureaus and bookshelves with baskets add lots of excellent storage to this space. The launching/landing pad is a critical space, but don't overthink it. Use the KISS method and find solutions that work for you.

Organizing Tip

Transitional space works best with the right storage. And choose the right storage for the item—coats on hooks, hats and gloves in baskets, sports equipment in bins—to make those baskets, buckets, and bags work for you.

In addition to hooks for hanging or quality hangers for the closet, the Three B's—baskets, buckets, and bags—create the right storage. Large baskets are great for any number of things—sports equipment, shoes, hats, mittens, you name it. Shallow buckets—with an emphasis on *shallow*—can serve the same purpose. If the bucket is too deep, you'll lose items at the bottom and will need to dump out the contents to find anything not visible on the surface. Think wide, not deep. And bags are a really versatile storage option in your transitional space. Check Target and HomeGoods for options on large, clothes baskets that can be hung on a hook to store gloves, scarves, and hats. Anything hung up uses the vertical space and keeps clutter from building on the floor and other horizontal surfaces.

> **CAVEAT: Whatever option you choose, start with safety. Be careful not to overload your storage so that it becomes a hazard, especially if you have "littles" in the home. They do love to tug and pull so be sure your solution isn't just about aesthetics and passes the safety test as well.**

And don't forget the shoes! Traditional shoe racks are great but if space is at a premium, a large basket works for corralling these items that seem to multiply at our entryways. A boot tray is a must in wet and snowy weather.

In this space, store items like bags, backpacks, and coats to keep from cluttering up the kitchen and other areas of the house. If you contain these items in one space, this keeps them from "migrating" and getting misplaced. Dumping our stuff in a pile or on the floor doesn't make our transitional space work—it just makes another mess. Having multiple storage options makes transitional space work. The right storage helps us build better organizational processes and keeps our other spaces clutter free.

One of the most critical uses of transitional space is to house those items not just entering your home but those that need to leave it. To create a process around getting items out of your space and to its new "home," take it to the transitional space, put it in a bag (I love a small paper handle bag) and staple a sticky note to the bag. If the item is ready to go when you leave the house, the likelihood that it will go is much greater. Need to return an item to the store? Hang the bag (with the receipt inside) on the coat rack and bring it to the car on your next trip out. Soccer practice tomorrow? Prepare the bag the night before and put it in the launching/landing pad to head out in the morning.

There are lots of options to set up your launching/landing pad. Figure out what works best for you. Now let's talk about keeping your transitional space organized.

5

Making Transitional Space Work

"Do not fear mistakes—fear only the absence of creative, constructive, and corrective responses to those mistakes."

—**Stephen Covey, 7 Habits of Highly Effective People**

o you remember that song from *Sesame Street*? "One of these things is not like the others …" Believe it or not, it helps to keep that song in your head when you organize, and especially when focusing on transitional space. Because transitional space is generally right inside the home (or office), it becomes a dumping ground for all the stuff coming in and going out. It's not unusual to find tennis rackets next to snow boots or mittens next to beach towels because they've just been dumped there. The first step to organizing your transitional space is clearing out the junk.

I've worked with organizing clients for close to a decade. I have seen things in transitional spaces like mudrooms, garage entryways, and closets that would astound you. Dog cages for Spot who went to puppy heaven years ago. Athletic gear for littles who are now in college. Coats and jackets that don't fit. Boots and shoes long past their usefulness and wear date. Mittens and gloves missing a mate. Snow tubes in July. Flip flops in January … in New England. And why is it all there? Because we aren't intentional about what we put in that space and we pass through without curating and editing it.

Think about the old adage, "The secret to getting ahead is getting started." Remove what isn't needed in this space right now, for this season, and rehouse those items. Eliminate the junk and what needs to be either purged or stored somewhere else. This will open up the space and make entering and exiting less stressful.

Speaking of junk, what else did you dump in this space? Did you clean the trash out of the car on your way in? Great. But don't let that trash and junk linger in the mudroom. Most of us don't have space in the launching/landing pad for a trash barrel so move that right into the kitchen trash. Seems simple, right? But you'd be surprised that when you start to do your launching/landing pad maintenance how much you can just throw out. Once you get rid of the true junk and trash, focus on what else is lying around. In a home with young children, this can be a real challenge. Little ones come in with their hands full and drop everything when they enter the space. Create a routine of hanging up coats and backpacks and putting shoes away. Create an "inbox" for school items so these critical pieces don't get lost and can be sorted through later and not mixed in with the real trash.

Once the junk is out, decide what needs to come back in. The essentials for this space are those items you need to get out the door on a daily basis. Items like your workbag, backpacks, keys, everyday coats, and shoes should stay and most everything else should be housed elsewhere.

Take an opportunity to make a quick run through your transitional space. What immediately jumps out as not belonging? Which one of these things is not like the other? Immediately purge, remove, and rehouse this item in the appropriate space. The only items that should be housed in your transitional space are those you need to "grab and go" today. Any others should not become permanent fixtures. Are there items that need to leave the house? Bring them right out to the car. What's in those mystery bags dumped on the floor? Move them into the house or office and put the contents away, not down, immediately. Is there dry cleaning hanging in this space? Walk it right to the closet and finish the project. Find items to donate? Great! Put them right into your car to drop off for

Organizing Tip

The best way to keep transitional space organized is by being diligent about maintaining your organizational system. On a weekly basis, do a critical walk-through and clear out the clutter to maintain your organized transitional space.

donation. If you have LOTS to donate, many organizations will pick up right at your home or office.

The good news is that clearing out that space and cleaning up the mess is easier here than in most other spaces. Space like basements, garages, and attics are large, open spaces that have less structure. With your transitional space, it's a much smaller, more defined space with fewer storage spots. What "lives" in your launching/landing pad are those things you *need* to get yourself out of your home or office each day; therefore the number of things that should remain in that space is limited.

What is one of the most important items we always need and should be stored in the transitional space? The keys. Oh, the crisis of the lost keys … is there a person who hasn't run around looking for the car keys to get out of the house, all the time shouting about "someone else" having moved the keys? If there is an organizing crisis that most people can relate to, it's definitely this one. Getting out of the home or office with less stress is always the goal. Storing important items, like keys, in the transitional space will make this a lot easier.

If grabbing the keys and going is your goal, there are two simple solutions to this organizing crisis. My favorite solution is a simple key rack installed by the door. Hanging up the keys means that they are clearly visible and easy to access—grab and go. Strongly urge everyone in the home to leave the keys in the launching/landing pad. This will come in very handy when you need to move cars around in the driveway or use a different car—one spot, one solution.

When you are installing a key rack, also think about height, especially with "littles." When my younger son was about three, he loved anything shiny, especially "Daddy" things. I have a very vivid memory of turning the house upside down at 5:30 a.m. when my husband could not find his keys because my son had put them in his "secret spot." That said, aim high when installing the rack.

A second option, which some clients prefer, is a bowl for the keys. When you enter the house, drop the keys in the bowl in the transitional space and grab them on the way out. Having a bowl or small basket for the keys is a great option for your office as well. No more guessing or patting down all your pockets or rummaging through your briefcase, work bag, or purse for the car keys. Either solution is great—provided you use it! Do not carry the keys farther into the house or office and then deposit them on the kitchen table, countertop, or other surface. This is a surefire way to be searching for those keys the next time you need to get out the door.

Organizing Tip

Out of sight means out of mind. If we store important items like keys in the transitional space, they will never (likely) be lost again.

Your launching/landing pad is a critical part of your home organization—it's the space that gets you in and out, likely multiple times a day. Keeping that space organized is to make that transition easier.

6

But My Organizing Challenge Is Unique!

"For being different, it's easy. But to be unique, it's a complicated thing."

—**Lady Gaga**

Over the years, I've given a number of seminars and workshops on organizing as well as working with individual clients. I love sharing the work I do and I especially love hearing about and trying to solve organizing challenges. Everyone has some sort of unique organizing challenge. Maybe it's physical layout; maybe it's a family member's special physical or emotional needs; maybe it's a strong aesthetic desire. Because of this, finding the right storage solution needs to be unique to the situation and intuitive to you. Julie Morgenstern called this "organizing from the inside out" and talks about this process in her excellent book on the subject.

In addition to the classic complaint of "not enough space" is the challenge of volume. Volume, volume, volume. Our hyper-driven, consumer culture has led to a volume of stuff that is unprecedented. And it's not just ourselves we're buying for; this phenomenon has absolutely trickled down to our children. We love our kids. We want them to have the best of everything, all the stuff our parents couldn't afford to buy for us. That's a generous and loving concept. The challenge lies in the result of those sentiments. *So much stuff.* Kids' rooms and playrooms and the resulting spillover into other areas of the home traditionally considered "adult" space is at an all-time high.

I've done a lot of work in this area and while there are the common themes of volume, storage, and space, there are some unique organizational situations to manage. Can you guess one of the most unique challenges? If you said something that's round, bouncy, and seems to multiply overnight in homes with children, you'd be right. Balls. Balls everywhere. Balls pose a unique organizing challenge because containerizing them is critical. Finding the right solution is about more than aesthetics; it's really about safety. More times than I can count, I've stepped into a hallway or room to find an array of baseballs, basketballs, volleyballs, beachballs, and everything in between crowding the space and making a hazard of walking. And that's just in my own home. As the parent of two sons who played baseball, basketball, football, and soccer, I've picked up and put away more balls than I even want to think about. So, when I work with my clients, this is a challenge that I can really relate to.

Barbies, baby dolls, and their many accessories—not so much—but the concept is the same and the solutions are similar. These smaller items seem to multiply overnight and because singularly they don't take up a lot of space, we can miss seeing the clutter they become in volume.

Like the errant pine needles and holiday ornament I randomly find in July, balls and Barbies also have amazing "sticking" power. We don't want to just throw them out. (What if the neighbors' kids come over? Or your cousin visits with his little kids?) So,

Organizing Tip

For a reader without children in the home, you are not immune to this overwhelming phenomenon. Sports and fitness equipment as well as electronics— grown-up "toys"— are a challenge for many to store and organize. Determining the best storage for those particular items is key.

we keep them. In our space. And after a certain point, we stop "seeing" them altogether. They become clutter that has overwhelmed the space because we are no longer using and enjoying them. "Not what we have but what we enjoy, constitutes our abundance." Epicurus said this in the third century BC, and it is even more accurate today. We need to focus our attention on this particular organizing challenge to start to get rid of the volume of clutter.

Organizing Tip

Pick a spot—
playroom, mudroom,
bedroom—wherever
a multitude of an
item has amassed
and get started.

Set the timer on your phone for 60 or 90 minutes (or another realistic time frame.) Move from space to space focused only on a specific item wherever it's housed. Don't get sidetracked with other priorities or organizing—focus on the toys, books, piles of paper—whatever unused item is taking up the most space and volume. You'll be amazed at what you can accomplish in a short time. Warning! It's best to do this task alone unless you feel you need input from others on what to keep and what should go.

Is your family still using these items? Great. Sort through the volume, throw out or donate the unused ones and then figure out where to best store the remainder and containerize them. Have "the kids" headed to college and these items are gathering dust and taking up valuable square footage in your space? Purge these items immediately and open up that space. If toys and sports equipment is in good, usable condition, give them new life. Check out the Where to Donate Anything section at the back of the book or find a local charity for donating these and other items.

Now that you have the "right" amount to keep, how do you control the chaos? Again, pick a storage option that works for that particular item—this is not a "one solution fits all" scenario. For balls, large shallow baskets and bins are the ideal storage solution. Think wide, not deep, so items below the top layer are easy to get to and don't get lost in the bottom. Your right storage solution should be placed in a convenient, easy to access spot. The garage, the mudroom, the basement—pick the storage spot that is intuitive and works for you. If these are balls (or other toys) that are often used outside, keep them near or in your launching/landing pad so kids can "grab and go" to head outside to play. When the kids come back in, the ball goes back into the container and it's ready for the next time. (I don't recommend storing most toys outside if they are uncovered. Rain and snow result in mildew and the quality deteriorates. If you don't have good storage in your transitional area, try a covered bin for your outside items. Resin is cost-effective and good at keeping the elements out.) If Barbies and dolls are your organizing nemesis, shallow bins and baskets work really well. Choose one for the dolls and one for the many, many accessories.

If you concentrate on what you have, you'll always have more. That's the abundance mindset. If you concentrate on what you don't have, you'll never have enough and you'll constantly be trying to accumulate more. This scarcity mentality keeps us from seeing the abundance that already exists in our life and adds to the volume and clutter in the home. The example of toys and balls is an apt one, but the same systems and solutions are valid for many, many items. Crafting supplies, clothes, tools, shoes, electronics, books— all of these are items that easily accumulate and become difficult for us to manage and then part with. Repeat the same process—purge, containerize, and create a home—for any group of items that has reached critical volume. Space is finite; limit your volume.

Whenever I give a talk or presentation, another of the most common questions is, "How do I organize all the Legos?" Because of the sheer volume of Legos, there needs to be an organizational system for both storage and display. The good news is that there are lots of options—both for completed kits as well as the parts.

Legos are a wonderful way to learn spatial, engineering skills. It can challenge a budding engineer or architect to create something completely new and unique or follow instructions to complete a kit. We owned many kits; Harry Potter and Star Wars themes were a huge hit in our house. As a parent and organizer, the greatest struggle is how to containerize and manage sets that are in progress and loose pieces.

Like balls, Legos need to be containerized both for use and safety. Kits and projects cannot be completed if pieces are missing so keeping the pieces together is important. And stepping barefoot on a Lego? Painful and dangerous.

For a great storage solution, look down. Shallow, under bed storage boxes have the width to contain low sets and the loose pieces that litter the floor and make walking a hazard. As a bonus, these under bed storage boxes slide easily out of sight for quick clean up. If you have floor space, a freestanding bin system is a great organizational tool but simple plastic bins, ideally with lids, also work well. Some LEGO lovers prefer to color code and separate their pieces. If that's the case, free-standing bin systems and plastic bins work best.

So, once the kits or project are completed, now what do I do with all the LEGO creations? Looking to display some planes, spaceships, and other wonderful flying machines? Look up!

Organizing Tip

Another option for kits and their pieces is to store them by set. You don't have to keep the pieces in those flimsy cardboard boxes that fall apart, allowing pieces to "escape." Cut out the photo on the box so your junior engineer has a visual reference and then stick it in with the pieces. I love an XXL zip top bag with the kit name written on the front. Again, clear plastic bins with all the pieces and the photo taped on the top or included in the box also works. The key is containerizing the pieces for use and storage.

A simple C-Hook screwed into the ceiling and some fishing wire will make a great display. This works particularly well with aerial/flying creations, but can work for other modes of transport as well. More constructed sets and scenes? Again, look up and use the vertical space in the room. Adding extra shelves moves these creations up and out of reach and makes an ideal display space and keeps the sets intact. Remember, space is a finite thing. We can only store and display a certain number of items. Horizontal spaces that are covered with creations and treasures can quickly become cluttered and unusable.

Truth be told, I love being "stumped" by my clients with an organizing challenge. If it's a totally new experience or challenge, or one you've been struggling with, I recommend sitting with the project and not diving right in. Sometimes it takes processing, and some trial and error, to find the right solution.

Organizing a Collector

S. and I started working together after he had made a
recent move. A good friend of mine had helped him move
into his current apartment across the city and the move
included dozens of boxes **unopened** from a previous move
four years prior. Yup. Four years of living amidst boxes
housing the many beautiful things he had accumulated in
his travels and throughout his successful life. I'd like to think
my clients have learned a thing or two from me over the
years but I know I've learned a lot from them. And from
S., I learned about model cars (and Nambe, crystal, and a
myriad of other, beautiful things…).

My first question to him was not, "How do you want
this space to look?" or "Where do you want to put all your
things?" Instead the question was "How do you want to
live?" Our goal was to eliminate all the things he really was
never going to use again—bigger homes, different life—and
incorporate those things that were most important. From
there, we created an action plan to focus on displaying and
storing those items that really had value to him: his artwork,
family pictures, and his prized car collection. My client has
hundreds of model cars, which he loved, and displaying
the best of the collection was an important goal. He could
recite the model, make, and intricate details of each car
from memory—it was a joy to see the pleasure he found in
these cars! His apartment was modern and wall space was
limited to maximize windows and light. This did not leave

(continued)

us with many options for displaying the cars aside from traditional display boxes which were bulky and took up a lot of horizontal space which was already minimal.

One design element that was underutilized was a long narrow hallway with fairly high ceilings. How could we use this physical space to our advantage without adding bulk to the walls, which would make the walking space too narrow? We looked up, installing narrow plastic display shelving intended for retail store display. We lined the hallway and the spare bedroom with this clear shelving as close to the ceiling as was feasible and created a car "runway." Brilliant, if I do say so myself! The visual was really impactful because it was so unique and unexpected and gave him the "wow" factor he was going for. In the words of Milton Glaser, "There are three responses to a piece of design—yes, no, and wow! Wow is the one to aim for." For a couple hundred dollars, we created a custom display solution that combined volume and aesthetics. Win/win.

We're still learning from each other, S. and I. We get together monthly for "maintenance sessions"; I still have a lot to learn about art and he's still working on his organizing....

Every space and item is unique in its own way. Recognize that the organizing needs and the right storage solutions need to adapt to meet those needs. Think intuitively about how you want to use the items to figure out the right storage solution.

7

It's Not the Box or the Bin

"Perfection of means and confusion of goals seem to characterize our age."

—**Albert Einstein**

Since starting my organizing practice, I have had the privilege of working with some of the kindest, generous, and most amazing clients. Through our work, they have transformed their lives and their spaces. These clients came to me because for many people, getting organized is a challenge. Allowing another person into your space requires real strength to set aside any embarrassment and ask for help. Sometimes it takes us months or years before we get to that point of frustration, and we realize we are ready to make a change in any area of our lives: health and wellness, financial security, relationships, or organization. To create that success, we need to make the changes necessary to bring about long-term success. "The successful person has the habit of doing things failures don't like to do. They don't like doing them either necessarily. But their disliking is subordinated to the strength of their purpose."[4]

Unfortunately, there's a misconception that—with just the right products—we can buy that success. The products that we buy can be tools to achieving the ends we desire, but they do not and cannot substitute for doing the work. Many times when I first meet with a client, I'll be handed organizational products—bins, boxes, filing systems—and clients are mystified as to why after buying these products, they couldn't organize themselves. But the reality is that getting organized isn't about the box or the bin; it starts with "why I want to get organized" and moves into having the "right stuff" in our spaces.

In life, you can't buy organization any more than you can buy beauty, or happiness, or success. Or in the words of the musician Travis Scott, "You can't buy vision and you can't buy aesthetic." You can try to purchase the trappings of all those things, which is what our consumer culture wants us to believe. That we can buy our way to happiness, something that has led to a culture of debt, depression, and discontent. In his book *Authentic Success*, Robert Holden talks about how we have a false sense of success, surrounded by all these empty trappings. "To be successful in life, work and relationships, you have to do one thing first—you have to show up." We have to show up in our lives every day, in our space, and work toward the goals we've said are important. There are no shortcuts, no life hacks, no easy way out, but the value and the gift of living a truly intentional life is immeasurable.

Focusing on "why I want to get organized" is first. Part of understanding the "why" is defining what organizing means to *you*. I define organizing as "finding my stuff when I need it"—that's it. For you, it might mean getting out of the house in the morning without stress. Or picking clothes out of your closet that fit and make you look and feel fabulous. Or entertaining in your home with joy and excitement. Whatever your goals and definition for organization, you can't jump ahead to products and systems. Believe it or not, solutions and creating systems is the easy part. The more challenging part, which you cannot skip, is defining your goals and then doing the actual work. Stephen Covey, in his highly acclaimed book *7 Habits of Highly Effective People,* spends a lot of time on this premise. He stresses the importance of taking responsibility for the actions that drive success and the effort that is required. "Happiness can be defined, in part at least, as the fruit of the desire and ability to sacrifice what we want now for what we want eventually."

Things will get harder before they get easier. To make things better, sometimes we first have to make a mess. I warn all of my clients about this. It is imperative to recognize that you first have to determine what your goal is and then focus on the "doing of the doing." Clients often want to dig right in where they are with high hopes for success. But truly understanding the challenges and creating an effective plan are the critical first steps to success. President and General Dwight D. Eisenhower is quoted as saying, "Plans are worthless but planning is everything," and I agree completely.

As an organizing coach, I help clients articulate and create a vision for organizing and living their best life. Is being organized a launching/landing pad that gets you in and out of your space with minimal stress and time? Is being organized feeling less stressed by tasks and projects and in better control of your time and space? How do you want to feel in your space? How do you want to live every day? Often when a client has lived with a level of disorganization for a period of time, they are unable to envision a solution or "see the forest through the trees."

On a number of occasions when I've asked a client, "What's your organizing vision?" I've been handed a magazine spread with a perfectly organized playroom, family room, bedroom, etc. The scene is picturesque, the white furniture (for some reason the furniture is always white!) positioned just so, no clutter, no mess and it looks perfect. And as I hand the magazine back to the client, I say quite gently, "That's lovely, but that's a story. That's not real life." Because real life is messy. It has Legos, Barbies, books, crayons, dirty laundry, sports equipment, papers and files, and electronics all around the space—because that's real life. Embrace the mess and the reality because that's where the magic happens. Don't focus on trying to create a "perfect scenario" because the cost in terms of stress, frustration, and resources is prohibitive. In that respect, the journey is not worth the destination.

Once I understand what a client is trying to accomplish, we can work together to create a plan to manifest that vision. Effective, intuitive organizing starts with a vision, not a product or process. Any good project starts with the "why" and not the "how" or "what." The saying is "Ten minutes of planning is worth 60 minutes of work"—and that is super helpful when thinking about organizing. Clients often want to jump into a certain project without working out an overall plan, or to get to the prize, but that can lead to more frustration. So, how do you create your vision for organizing?

Stay focused on the day-to-day. I see clients who want to focus on how they will entertain at Thanksgiving and the holidays and plan around that but neglect the impact on everyday living. Create a plan that meets your needs 90 percent of the time; the other 10 percent and

Organizing Tip

To create your vision for organizing, ask, "What's my greatest challenge?" Or stated another way, "What's my biggest pain point? What area(s), when organized, would have the greatest impact on my everyday life to reduce my stress and improve day to day functioning?"

special occasions and situations you can adapt to. If you don't need a guest room except for ten to fifteen days out of the year, don't dedicate that much space to that small percentage of time and usage. The space is much better utilized as an office or playroom with a daybed; or create a multiuse space that has greater impact on the bulk of your time.

To get started, pick the most impactful place(s) and prioritize from there. Priorities often shift once organizing starts, and plans need to be flexible enough to accommodate changing needs. To help my clients drill down on this, I ask, "If I had a magic wand and I could "fix" three things in your space, what would they be?" This magical thinking is a great starting point because it allows us to be creative. Often some of the best solutions have come from getting outside the box and implementing non-traditional systems and solutions.

Caveat: A caveat to this magical thinking: There are no shortcuts in organizing; you still have to commit time and resources to doing the work.

Another common theme I've seen over the years with clients is the perception of where the challenge or bottleneck occurs. A client might state that, "I can't get us out of the house in the morning because my mudroom is a mess." Well, maybe that's the case. But it could also be that your closet and wardrobe are really the sticking points—leading to stress and frustration that make the morning exit a daily struggle. Be open to seeing things in a new light. Or as Stephen Covey said, "The way we see the problem is the problem."

Are you ready to take the next step? I hope you said "yes!" Purging is the next step in the organizing process to get rid of the excess—the damaged, the unused, the unneeded. Some offices will benefit from two copy machines and maybe even two coffee makers. Some families do better with a streamlined approach to toys and books; others thrive with a multitude of options. The reality is that in our manic society we have personal space deprivation and a hyper, active workplace. We need to create space that allows us to de-stress, unwind and find peace, creativity, and productivity. Customize the solutions that truly work for you—there is no "right way" or "right number/amount" when it comes to organizing, and be leery of anyone that tells you different. To quote *Hamlet*, "... for there is nothing either good or bad, but thinking makes it so."

Ready to get going and purge? Hold on tight; it's going to be a bumpy ride....

8

Where Does All This Stuff Live?

"True wisdom is letting go of what is not valuable in order to be with what is priceless."

—Robert Holden

The concept of "less" that can change your life is less stress, less worry, less anxiety, and less debt. Work toward less frustration, less negativity in our relationships, and less feeling trapped in your financial instability and clutter-filled homes. When you look at it this way less really can be more. More space, more time, more joy in our lives....

The shift from seeing "less" as a negative to a positive happens when we embrace the idea that our lives are more open and freer when we are not bogged down by our "stuff." And that's not just the physical stuff. That's the mental, emotional, and psychological stuff that clutters our lives and keeps us from living intentionally and fully.

When it comes to managing your physical space—home or office—less is definitely more. Most people struggle with "why should I let it go?" and then get bogged down in the where and the how. Before getting stuck in the weeds of the details, first focus on, "What should I let go and what should I keep?" The answer that I suggest for my clients, and the one I live by, is simple. The two things you should have in your space are things you need and things you love; everything else should go.

Working with an organizer has a number of benefits to getting an organizing project done. An organizer does not have the emotional attachment to the items that you may have. This objectivity allows an organizer to provide constructive and helpful feedback on what should stay and what might go. Note: you may have an organized, well-meaning friend or family member who wants to help you with the purging and

Organizing Tip

If letting go of items, i.e. purging, is a challenge for you, now is the time to bring in a professional organizer or organizing coach. We help our clients see "the forest through the trees" and get to the heart of what needs to get done. You can find a productivity and organizing professional through the National Association of Productivity & Organizing Professionals at NAPO.net.

decluttering. While this is a wonderful sentiment, this has the potential to set an unhealthy and unproductive dynamic. When clients suggest having a friend or family member "help," 95 percent of the time I decline (unless we're dealing with a move or another big project). The reason? The organizer/client relationship is a professional relationship. We know the questions to ask to get you to make your best decisions about what to keep, what to let go, and how to set up your space. A family member may have a personal and emotional attachment similar to your own or may not be sensitive at all to the emotional components of the process.

Because we have experience in similar situations, we can help you customize a plan that will be most effective for you. Have you tried to get organized on your own in the past but the project stalled? Professional organizers and coaches are also invaluable in keeping clients motivated and on task.

Most of us accumulate "stuff" over the years so the first question to ask is: "Do I *really* need it?" Should I let go of a waffle iron if I never make waffles or a beer making kit if I don't drink beer? Let it go—donate it and move it on. The number of groups and organizations that will take donated items in almost any area is enormous—find a list of resources for donating some common items in the appendix. The mixer and blender we use every day? Find appropriate counter space and make using these items easier. Figure out what's an important part of your daily "flow" and incorporate those items. Don't take up your prime real estate with seldom used items. This space should be dedicated to your day-to-day. For the seldom used, but still needed items like holiday, party, etc.—store these in an alternate space like the basement if possible.

The second question to ask is: "Do I love it?" The china we've inherited from Grandma and really love? Find a way to display it, use it, and enjoy it. The painting your former boyfriend's mother gave you and you never really liked? Let it go—maybe someone else has just that right wall space to fill. The two things we should have in our home are things we need and things we love. You need your vacuum cleaner and your slow cooker so you keep them. You love your antique glassware and shell collection—keep them because looking at them brings you joy. Alternatively, if looking at something makes you cringe: Let it go. It's taking up negative physical, mental, and emotional space in your life. Stuff cannot make you happy, but it can make you unhappy. George Carlin said it in a way that was easy to picture. "Trying to be happy by accumulating possessions is like trying to satisfy hunger by taping sandwiches all over your body." Find the happiness inside you; that's where it lives. Keep the joy; let the rest go.

When we start organizing a space, the volume can be over-whelming and, well, surprising sometimes. To determine the true number or volume of the category you are organizing, start by gathering them up so you can decide on how many you really need to keep. Surprised by how many of this item you own? Don't be. You were doing your best in the moment so don't beat yourself up about it. We live in a consumer-driven culture where buying is a preoccupation and a hobby. Forgive yourself about your overspending and overbuying. Use this as an opportunity to change your present and your future.

Purging what you already have starts the process. This is where we start with every organizing project—getting rid of the excess, the unneeded, and the unused. Once you have the items you want to move out of your space, now what do you do with all this stuff? Donating is a wonderful choice. You get the space back and help someone else in the process. And donating your unneeded and unused items couldn't be easier—see the list of resources on how to donate just about anything at the back of the book.

Be mindful about what you put aside for donation and what should be thrown away. If an item is in unusable condition— dirty, stained, broken beyond simple repair—err on the side of caution and put it in the trash. Recycle everything you can before adding to the garbage or landfill. Books, magazines, and even mismatched playing cards and incomplete board games and the like can usually be put in paper or cardboard recycling. Plastic items like stained and mismatched plastic containers and plastic toys can often be recycled depending on your local recycling guidelines. If clothing and linens are still in decent condition, put them in the donation pile. Often charities sell cloth items in bulk for recycling so be mindful before anything gets thrown in the trash.

I've noticed a number of trends with clients, including when clients decide to start working with me. Often working with an organizer is triggered by a life transition. Hopefully, the transition is a positive one: new home, new baby, new work opportunity. Other times, clients are faced with transitions after the illness or passing of a loved one, physical or emotional struggles, work challenges, and other life changes. The theme of many of these transitions is that systems that once worked have "broken down" and clients are faced with situations and *stuff* that suddenly (or not so suddenly) feels overwhelming. My response is to slow down, take a deep breath, and create an effective plan. Think about your overall organizing goal, and start by tackling those spaces and items that will have the highest impact.

So, what are some of the most high-volume and high-impact items in our space? Toys and books. These are two of the greatest organizing challenges in terms of volume. Are toys and kid books taking up space and gathering dust now that "the kids" are now adults? Donate to Big Brothers/Big Sisters to be reused and re-loved. Learning-to-read books are especially valued by organizations that serve children and their families. VA hospitals and care facilities appreciate good condition books for adult readers; mysteries, non-fiction, and biographies are always popular.

Repurposing, reusing, and recycling—that's the mantra for making your purging and donating process viable. Even though you may not see an immediate need or value in an item to be donated, trust me that there is likely an organiza-

Organizing Tip

I know that it can be difficult to part with books. Clients and I spend a lot of time going through book collections to pare down to "reasonable" amounts. Be realistic. If your pile of books "to be read" numbers over twenty, review your pile again. That's a lot of books. The same goes for books you plan to reread. Are there some classics you want to reread some day? Sure; keep a couple. If your bookshelves are sagging under the weight of unread books, seriously consider donating some today.

tion that is thrilled to receive your donations. Prom and bridesmaid dresses get to see the dance floor again when you donate them to organizations that create special events for differently-abled young adults and high schoolers who cannot afford to buy a dress. Household items you'll never use make a house a home for another family in new or transitional housing. All of those unused and unneeded items that are taking up your space can make a world of difference for another person. Think also about specific people who might need an item. A niece moving into her first apartment? Maybe she'd love those extra pots and pans, but get them

Organizing Tip

First ask if someone would like the items you are donating—do not assume. Do not get rid of your excess by dumping it on someone else. Also, if at all possible, get the item to them immediately. Holding onto items for "future" donations just adds to your clutter and disorganization.

to her right away. Furniture, bedding, lamps, decorative items you've loved but are now ready to move on can save a lot of money and hassle for someone else.

Over the years, I have seen clients encounter a number of roadblocks to letting go of items cluttering their space. Sometimes, we experience guilt over moving items along because they were a gift from someone special. We feel "bad" about not keeping the item, whether or not we like it or need it. We would rather risk clutter and disorganization than feel or appear disloyal. This guilt compounds into indecision and you are unable to move forward. Often, it's easier to blame others for why we can't clear out the clutter because "they," the nameless, faceless "they," will be upset. But getting organized requires—demands actually—that you focus on your actions and what you can and must do for yourself. In his book, *7 Habits of Highly Effective People*, Stephen Covey states it very clearly. "It is so much easier to blame other people, conditioning or conditions for our stagnant situation. But we are responsible—response-able—to control our lives and to powerfully influence our circumstances by working on being, on what we are."

When we are unable to part with a gift, often it's because we allow ourselves to believe that possessions are an embodiment of the giver. In this scenario, objects take on feelings and sentiments. Instead of helping us or bringing us joy, they become a source of guilt and negative emotions. When this happens, we need to stop and reassess our perspective. You love Grandma and she loves you; her gift of the china was just that—a gift. You receive, and give, a gift with an open hand; it is not yours or anyone else's right to say how it should be received or used.

Many times clients have asked me for permission to get rid of items that have been given to them. You don't need my permission or anyone else's to declutter your space. As a courtesy, you can ask others in your family or circle of friends if they have need of a particular item. "I no longer have space for this great *fill in the blank*. Do you or anyone else you know need this? I'd love to find it a 'good home.' " We all want to feel that our donated items will be appreciated and well loved but if finding just the right donation place is holding you back, this has become a roadblock for you. As Marie Kondo says so succinctly in her book *The Life-*

Changing Magic of Tidying Up: The Japanese Art of Decluttering and Organizing, "Thank it for its service and let it go."

Another major roadblock I find with my clients is the belief that: *Since I've paid a lot of money for X, then I should hold onto it or at least sell it to recoup some of the cost.* I have coached many clients through this scenario and it can be tricky for a number of reasons. The reality is that just because you paid a lot of money for this table, this phone, this dress, does not necessarily mean that someone else will pay an equivalent amount for it. Especially with items that had a hefty price tag, we often want to recoup some of the expense. So, how do you determine what it's worth?

Inherently, there are two different kinds of value. Intrinsic worth is the value something has in itself, i.e. a mixer. Fifteen years ago you bought this mixer; you used it a lot and it was very helpful and handy at one point. This has a lot of *intrinsic* value to you. The market worth or value is different. The *market price* is what "the market" will pay for this item today, right now, in its current condition. If you loved and used an item, it has served its intrinsic value well. An item's resale worth is likely going to be much less than what you paid, but the outcome of opening up your space is absolutely greater.

Still want to sell your item? Be open and realistic. In the years since you've purchased that item, a number of upgrades or newer models have been released. Remember, our consumer-driven culture perpetuates the message that we must have the latest and greatest of everything. Sure, that fifteen-year-old mixer works great and still has value. But, in truth, why would I buy Mixer Version 1.0 when I can purchase Mixer Version 9.0

Organizing Tip

If you are trying to determine an item's market price, eBay is a great resource. eBay has one of the best pricing algorithms available due to the sheer volume of items for sale on its site.

for close to the same cost? There's a reason we had the iPhone X in ten years. It's not because we need that many upgrades; it's because we believe we need the most recent upgrade and model. With electronic items especially, change and upgrading happens so rapidly items purchased just a couple of years ago lose significant value quickly as a "newer and better" model or two hits the market.

Okay. What if you believe that your item still has real value? Slightly used electronics, designer clothes, and high-end home items fall in this category. Local online yard sales and resellers can net you some cash if you have the time and inclination to resell your items. There are a number of online retail sites that specialize in reselling high-end designer goods.

> **Caveat: High end resale sites, like TheRealReal. com and Rebagg.com accept only true designer items in pristine condition. You will have to prove authentication so you need to have original sales receipts, etc. If you received these as a gift or purchased through a third party, this can be challenging. Be realistic about the value of your item and what you might receive.**

When calculating what you might net for your sale, remember to add in the time that it will take you to resell your item. I've had the opportunity to resell items for clients on a number of occasions, but when you add in the time your organizer will charge to resell your item, it often doesn't make economic sense. If your item is very high-end—think home furnishings—it might be worth it to invest your time in getting this sold. Do some research into furniture consignment options in your area. Or decide to donate and forgo the cash for the tax deduction. There are so many organizations that would gladly take your donations so you'll need to weigh the true cost of selling or donating.

For most of us, we have things that we value highly for a number of reasons: purchase price, sentimentality, rarity, etc. As you go through your purging process, put aside the items that you might want to resell versus donate, and focus first on your donations. Moving donation items out immediately will open up a lot of space so you can focus on the much smaller number of items to be sold. Control your stuff; don't let your stuff control you.

Clients have come to me over the years through a number of sources: a seminar, a speaking engagement, a referral, the NAPO website, my blog, etc. And while each client has been distinct and unique in goals and challenges, with each client I always have focused on the same process and overarching goal: How do I live my best life? Knowing that I will die (and yes, this is the reality for all of us), how do I want to live? Do I want to live a stressed, frazzled life, bouncing from one crisis to another, buried under clutter and things? Or do I want to live a life of intention and purpose, in peaceful surroundings with the things I need and love? To achieve that end—more space, more time, and more joy—I coach my clients to "be the goal." If you want organization, be organized. You generate possibility through example so you need to start somewhere. All things are in motion in our lives and we have an opportunity to create the life we want. Through intentional living and organization, we can let go of the clutter and open up space for a better life.

9

What Is Good Storage and an Effective System?

"Life is really simple but we insist on making it complicated."

—**Confucius**

ull disclaimer: I am a true organizing geek. I *love* organizing books, magazines, and articles; before and after photos of organizing are a bit of an obsession. Pinterest is a personal black hole of organizing pins. The Container Store catalog is like candy to an organizer so I understand the love of purchasing organizing products. But remember, that's just a product; it's not a solution to your organizing challenge.

Organizing is a process, not an event. When you decide to live an intentional life and incorporate organization into your spaces, this will be an ongoing task. There is no "one and done" with organizing. You need to choose products and create systems that work for you and then maintain those systems and habits. Lewis Howes put it this way: "True greatness comes from the intentional act of doing something positive over and over and over again." When we focus on our every day choices, we create the life we want to live.

Once you've purged and determined what's going to remain in your space, you need to decide on how it's going to be stored. If it's a big item, like furniture, it's likely going to be self-contained and take up floor space (a very valuable commodity!). Most other items, however, will be stored within other containers. Think clothes in a dresser; dishes and glassware in cabinets; books in the bookcase; and linens and towels in a closet. These are simple, easy-to-determine storage solutions because the items we are containing are straightforward, i.e. dishes in the cabinet. But for many

Organizing Tip

Note that "the best storage option" is the one that meets 90 percent of your needs and is cost-effective as well. Sometimes a cardboard box marked with a Sharpie is the best storage option. You don't need expensive bins and containers most of the time. Use what you already have and repurpose.

other things that fill our homes and offices, the choices are more varied, and this is where we need to choose the best storage option available.

Clear plastic shoe boxes work really well for arts and crafts, small toy items, school and office supplies and so many other items. The bonus of these small, clear bins is that they are stackable—doubling and tripling your storage space. When choosing storage items think KISS—Keep It Seriously Simple—because it's not about the box or the bin. Don't over-think or overcomplicate it.

Good storage is easy to use, easily accessible, and meets your price point. I recommend a variety of storage options based on the items you need to contain. I am a huge proponent of

Organizing Tip

When you choose a storage solution, think about trying to find that item when you are looking for it. Being able to "see" it is key, not only for yourself but for family members and co-workers. Don't waste time having to search through a multitude of boxes and bins for the one thing you are looking for. I suggest choosing a clear storage option whenever possible unless you are really trying to hide items from view. Opaque is not your friend! Some clients like color-coded tubs for holiday decorations. Red-and-green tubs for Christmas decorations and orange for Halloween and Thanksgiving make storing and finding your holiday items a lot easier. Conversely, fifteen unlabeled blue tubs will frustrate you and waste time when you are searching for something.

decanting items out of their original packaging into some-thing that works more efficiently. If the original storage is inconvenient, find another storage solution that works better. You don't have to keep the puzzle pieces in the original, broken and damaged cardboard box. Cut off the picture of the completed puzzle and slip it into a zip top bag with the puzzle pieces. Small toys and games, health and beauty items along with office supplies are great stored this way. Zip top bags are an organizer's best tool! Low cost, easy to use and putting items away is simplified.

Do you want to view your item and access it easily? Use clear, plastic bins with covers throughout your home and office. These bins come in a myriad of sizes and are great containers for office and school supplies, arts and crafts, medicines, and health and beauty items. You can utilize larger bins for storing off season clothing or bedding and take these items out of your everyday storage, opening up that critical real estate. Use these clear bins to corral small and loose items in any room including bathroom and kitchen.

Organizing Tip

Choose simple, sturdy products with good price points—good storage does not have to cost a lot. You can buy all of these at a home improvement or home goods store. In common spaces like the living room, aesthetics are more important, but this is not true of attics, basements, and other less visible space. You don't need to buy a fancy, high-end container system or fancy boxes or bins if a simpler solution works just as well.

Plastic storage bins and baskets are also ideal for organizing your cabinets and pantry. Do you have a multitude of boxes and cartons on the shelves and in the pantry? How often have you reached for the box of cereal only to find the nearly empty, now stale, remnants in the bag stuffed in the original box? With pantry items especially, organization is key. When you get home from the store, decant the cereal into a clear container so you know exactly how much you have and recycle the cereal boxes. Organizing these containers is a lot easier than managing different sized and shaped boxes. Remove the oatmeal packets, granola bars, and other prepackaged items into large zip top bags or clear bins so you know exactly what you have when you need it. That's what organizing is really about ... finding your stuff when you need it. Another bonus of using small, plastic bins and baskets is that you can wash them easily and keep your pantry cabinets clean and organized.

Organizing Tip

Searching for the best container for crayons? Remove them from that paper carton and put them in a clear Ziploc bag or basket. No more trying to cram them back into the original slots and ending up with broken magenta shards. Keep it simple and clear.

Use these clear containers to containerize categories so finding "like items" is easier. Target has a great line of organizing bins in a multitude of sizes. In the kitchen, group baking supplies, pancake supplies, and common cooking herbs and spices into these containers so cooking—and then clean up—is quicker. In the bathroom, put all your mani-cure items into one bin so it's easy to locate when you need it. As kids get older and start using their own specific products, invest in a portable shower caddy. This can be kept in the bedroom until needed and then brought into the bathroom. Then, everyone has his and her own product and the shower is not overflowing with a variety of different bottles. Ditto for cleaning supplies in a large caddy you can bring from room to room as you clean.

Spending time on the front end to create a system makes your life easier. When you buy something at the store, decant or organize it right then, don't wait! Yup, that's an organizing system. I have seen so many clients with bags and bags of stuff just sitting there—never put away, never used and forgotten about. If you deal with everything that comes into your space immediately, you will have more time on the back end when you need your items.

Remember the question I ask each client when I first meet them? "If I had a magic wand and could fix three organizing challenges, what would they be?" Organizing the attic and the basement are often on top of the list because they can become like the Wild West of disorganization.

Are you organizing and storing out-of-season or out-of-size clothing, extra linens, or holiday items? Extra large totes and tubs with locking covers are a great storage option for this space. These totes are waterproof and bug proof and as a bonus, they are stackable, thereby doubling or tripling your storage space. When you are choosing long-term storage containers, invest in good quality—don't skimp on this! Heat, humidity, and water are your greatest enemies when it comes to storage. It will get really hot in your attic and can get really wet in your basement—do not let the elements make your decisions for you about saving and storing your possessions.

Let's spend a few minutes talking about short-term versus long-term storage. It's a critical distinction and I've seen it impact many clients. Short-term storage is for items you need to access frequently—that seems pretty obvious. Because we need to use these items all the time, we need our storage to be easily accessible, versatile, and adaptable. When you're choosing a storage option, do you want the item to be viewable or hidden? Do you want to see the crayons and markers? Use a clear bin or open basket. (I have two sons in their 20s and I still have a basket of crayons, markers, and colored pencils for my nieces

Organizing Tip

Using extra-large, white labels from the office supply store, put one on each side of the container and mark with a permanent marker. If there's a label on each side, it doesn't matter how a tub is stacked or positioned—you'll always be able to read the label and know the contents.

and nephews to use when they visit. It is self-contained, in a cabinet but easily accessible.) Do you want to put books and toys in the family room but still want the space to appear uncluttered? Use a fabric bin or basket to "hide" the items for quick cleanup and storage. Think "outside the box"— pun intended—when you are thinking about storage. There is no right or wrong option—choose what works for you.

Some of the saddest situations I've seen have come from problems arising from ineffective, long-term storage. With good intentions, we rent a storage unit to be filled with furniture from past homes that won't fit or complement existing space. So you put it in a storage unit. And it sits. And you pay each month for it. If your present space is temporary, and I mean *really* temporary, with a solid date on the calendar, a storage unit is a good option. Be mindful and intentional about using long-term storage and don't use it as a dumping ground. Instead decide about your items and save yourself the physical and psychological space and money too.

When you are planning for long-term storage, whether in your own space or a storage unit, quality is so important! Again, spend the time on the front end. Put the decided upon items into the best storage you can afford—it will ultimately save money and heartbreak in the end. Cardboard moving and banker's boxes are not long-term storage solutions. You want the items you are storing to come out in the same condition as when you put them in and this, unfortunately, does not always happen. Humidity and moisture will break down these boxes quickly and make them structurally unsound and put your items at risk.

I have seen clients forced to throw out memorabilia, family photographs, designer clothing, electronics, and so much more that has been ruined in cardboard boxes. In addition to being a poor long-term storage choice, moving boxes allow us to defer our decisions about what to keep. We stack these boxes away and tell ourselves that one day, soon, we'll go through those boxes. I've worked with clients that had not gone through moving boxes from multiples moves and

Organizing Tip

I do not recommend that you just toss the box out, contents unseen, even if the boxes have been sitting for a number of years. I have worked with clients who did this previously and every time, they regretted it. The uncertainty and not knowing what might have been in that box is not a good feeling. Open the box, review the contents and then decide.

multiple years. So, if you haven't looked in that box in years, have no idea what's in it and haven't needed it by now, why are you keeping what's in there?

Go through each box doing what we call a "quick sort"— putting the contents into broad categories. Ninety percent of what's in those long-stored boxes is likely a donation, along with trash, but it is important to go through the box to see if it's something of personal or family value. Don't beat yourself up about not having dealt with this situation sooner or in another way. I continually remind my clients what my mother always told me: "What's done is done and we can't undo it. But we can learn from it and move on." Acknowledge that you could have handled it better and let go of the regret and guilt over the lost items and the lost money.

So what's the foolproof way to an effective system? For any organizing challenge, focus on creating a simple, easy-to-follow system. Lots of large toys to organize for your toddler? Consider low shelving with easy access and picture labels for pre-readers on baskets and bins. Lots of Barbies or Legos and Matchbox cars? Bins, bins, and more bins to the rescue to containerize. Are you struggling to get little ones out to school in the morning? Create transitional space with low hooks to hang coats and backpacks to make mornings more manageable.

I have found that some spaces are more challenging to organize. Smaller, more contained spaces—think pantries, closets, smaller rooms—are easier to organize because frankly, there are only so many options available. Space is a finite thing; you can't really create more of it. You can maximize the space you have by making good storage choices and finding "hidden" storage space. On the other hand, the vastness of a garage or basement gets people stuck because when there is more space, we fill it with more stuff. This is a negative, repetitive cycle we need to recognize and counteract; just because you have space, doesn't mean you have to fill it.

In larger, open spaces, break the space into zones—auto, holiday, seasonal, recreation—whatever categories your stuff falls into. Then choose the storage solutions and create the systems that are individualized and intuitive to you. Wire and plastic/resin rack systems are excellent choices in basements, garages, and even attics. They are sturdy, economical, and resistant to heat and moisture. Rack systems are easy to put together and can be done by one person. You can buy these at your local hardware or home store. Rack systems are also great because they store items up off the floor and can hold all kinds of boxes, bins, and tubs easily. Again, first we purge what needs to go and choose the storage option for what remains. Then create an organizing system. When you're devising your floor plan, use "the kindergarten method."

Think about how a kindergarten classroom is organized into zones: a reading area, art area, building area, desk area, etc. Set up your space the same way, filling in the "zones" that are specific to you.

Seasonal items like camping supplies, holiday, and other less frequently used items should be stored in the back and out of the way. Your goal is to know where these things are and get to them when you need them. You don't need Halloween decorations clogging up your prime real estate and sitting front and center in February. This is your space; you need to create the solution that works for you. Be flexible and try different options.

Organizing Tip

Keep more frequently used items within easy reach, especially if you are creating overflow pantry space. Be careful: This can become a dead zone of overbuying so be mindful about what you store here.

Organizing is an intuitive process. This is one of the first messages I share with an organizing client. Organizing must be intuitive to you and your family (or company) and must work in the context of your unique setting. From there, we create systems and solutions that address those unique and individual challenges. But what happens when "good systems" go "bad" and stop working? When we first move into a space, a new home, or an office, we set up our surroundings to meet our needs and everything goes great for a while. And then it seems that all of a sudden, as if overnight, things aren't working so well anymore. The mudroom or transitional space is a cluttered, jumbled mess. Instead of getting us out the door in a more efficient and less stressed way, it now adds to our frustration. Remember when you loved the layout of your closet and it was easy to pick out your wardrobe for the next day? Now, you can barely find anything and you feel "blah" when you finally get dressed. You spent so much *time* setting up the playroom. Why aren't the kids using that space anymore and now spreading toys all over the rest of your living space? So, what happened?

Even the best systems and solutions need to be adaptive to changing situations, both from a physical sense and a time perspective. Did the awesome filing system you created for your company fail to keep pace with your organization's growth? The result may be that the filing is now disorganized. Did the great toy solutions you created in your playroom for your toddler fail to keep pace with your child's more sophisticated electronics? So, how do I know if this system is no longer working for me?

As the old adage goes, "Don't throw the baby out with the bathwater." If a system or solution stops working, don't trash it—tweak it. High schoolers' backpacks don't fit in the little mudroom cubbies? Move hooks higher in a mudroom or transitional space to accommodate larger items and make the space more usable. Switch up baskets for bins which can hold bulkier items. Is your closet overflowing? Purge the unwanted and unneeded clogging up that space. We wear 20 percent of our clothes 80 percent of the time; there's likely a lot of unworn stuff taking up valuable real estate. In a playroom, remove small toy bins and open up shelving to accommodate larger toys and electronics. Weed through your files and shred old, unnecessary documents that you can reproduce online. Buy bigger filing cabinets to comfortably hold your necessary files and congratulate yourself on your company's growth.

Organizing systems need to be both adaptive and flexible to growth and change. Our situations change so our organizing solutions and systems need to keep pace.

Remember, this is not a "one and done." Consider your storage options and organizing solutions as organic systems that will grow and adapt as needed. Organizing is a process, not an event. I love this quote by Lewis Howes because it reminds me that sometimes we have to be really creative and more intuitive to find a solution that really works: "Failure is simply feedback. Use it and stay committed to your vision through taking action at all times. Don't stop now. Keep moving forward."

10

Maximizing My Space

"Whatever good things we build,
end up building us."

—Jim Rohn

etting up an effective storage system requires us to really think about our space in a new way.

To get to the nexus of an organizing challenge, I ask clients to walk me through the scenario of how the space is used. How often? By whom? What's working? What's not? This allows us to focus on the process, not the stuff or the space itself. Start with what does work; by focusing on the positive, we can build from there. It's unusual to find that there isn't something that works well in a particular space; start by focusing on what that something is. What can you build on or replicate from there?

Organizing Tip

This space planning process is similar to the time mapping that I coach clients through when we are focusing on "time management" and finding more time. The reality is that we can't truly manage time—that's a misnomer. What we can manage is how we use our time. We can also manage our actions and decisions which effect how we spend our time. (But more on that to come....)

Now that you've decided on what to keep, decide where the item should be stored—giving it a home. Please know that this is a highly intuitive process and a critical part of organizing! This is why when clients ask, "Can you organize me?" I always say, "No. But I can help you get organized." Every family and organization is unique. And every space is unique, so organize the space to meet your specific needs. In our home, we store the board games in the basement playroom. The kids could play down there with their friends and also easily bring the games to the kitchen or dining room to play as a family. In your home, the games might be stored in the toy room or family room because that works better for you.

Deciding on some items will be easier than others. It seems pretty obvious that dishes and glasses should be stored in the kitchen along with cookware. Toiletries in the bathroom? For some folks, this is the best solution but if space is limited, storing these items in adjoining or nearby space might be a better choice. Linens in the bedroom or hall closet? It depends. One of my favorite organizational tips came from my cleaning gal. She recommended keeping the bed linens in the room they were used in. With that, you don't have a mish-mash of sheet sets in a central closet and you're not trying to guess what is what and which set goes in what room. She also told me to fold up all the sheets and extra pillow cases and put them inside the pillow case; that way you have a full set of matching sheets all ready to go. Genius!

Books in the nursery or playroom? Likely both as well as other spots throughout the home. Be realistic when it comes to organizing. Yes, it would be ideal from a clutter perspective to keep all like items in one designated space or "home." But that's not real life. Your organization will be ineffective if you need to go to the playroom for a book every time you read a bedtime story to your child. That is not organization; that's inconvenience. Set up your space to work for you, not against you. Extra ink cartridges in the office supply

Organizing Tip

Store it where you use it. If you read in your bedroom 80 percent of the time, keep your books and magazines there. Do you paint and do arts and crafts at the kitchen table? Store the art supplies in or near the kitchen for easy access. Some items, like children's books and toys, will be in multiple locations. It is what it is. Designate a "home" for an item and return it there when you are done with it. That makes clean up and clearing clutter much easier. Start when your kids are very young; they learn systems quickly and easily and become self-sufficient when they can locate their own things.

Organizing Tip

Determine the right storage spot and return the item there when you are done using it or replenish/replace the used item right away. Did you use the last 60-watt light bulb? Write yourself a note to replace this as soon as possible. Do not rely on your memory to remember this next time you're at the store. If you wait until you need another, you will likely be in the dark, literally and figuratively, due to ineffective planning and organization.

closet? Great choice. But if the marketing department uses 80 percent of the ink in the office, keeping a supply in their space makes sense too.

If you are struggling to decide where to store an item (choosing its "home") ask, "Where do I use this most often?" If an item is used in multiple locations, ask, "Where would I think to look for this when I need it?" This is the very unique and intuitive part of the organizing process. I keep table-cloths and napkins in my dining room sideboard because we use them in that space. For you, storing these items in the linen closet or hall closet is more intuitive. If you are running around trying to remember or figure out where you stored something, that is poor organization. This is where the expression, "A place for everything and everything in its place," is most applicable.

How would you describe your storage space? If you have an older, vintage home like many in New England, you would likely describe your storage as limited. Likewise, I have a number of clients with amazing ocean and city views that trade closets and wall space for windows to enjoy the scenery. This is one of my favorite challenges: "creating" storage space. Maximizing your existing storage can take many forms including closet organizing, purging unneeded and unused items and choosing effective storage are important steps.

In organizing, good hiding spots equal effective space management. Common hiding spots are under the bed, behind a door, or even behind a floor length curtain. Behind full-length curtains in my office, I store a paper recycling bin and my shredder. They are available when I need them but I don't have to look at them either. You are really limited only by your imagination. These spots are ideal because they are not high traffic areas and are easily accessible.

The key to using hiding spots is that your decision is intentional. I have seen many clients who are overwhelmed by their possessions and the resulting clutter so they "hide" things away. They shove unopened mail in a drawer, documents in boxes, purchases they feel guilty about in closets and drawers. This is not what I am suggesting. I recommend that you choose a hiding spot based on how often you need to access the item and if it needs to be out and visible.

When we make intentional and thoughtful choices about our stuff, we maximize its use. I cannot count how many times, upon finding a "hidden" item that a client's reaction was, "Huh! I had forgotten about that." Or, "Wow! I was wondering where I put that!" This is not the reaction we are going for on a daily basis. Decide where you want your things to be stored so you can find them when you need them. That's organization in a nutshell.

Organizing Tip

I recommend creating an "electronics" bin for manuals, boxes, and warranties. I include information on cell phones, computers and printers, readers, tablets, etc. These items are costly so having the receipts and warranties and manuals handy for repairs and upgrades makes my life easier and saves me loads of time. I suggest keeping these separate from the rest of your manuals and warranties because they are needed much more frequently. Also, you don't need to clog up your everyday, working files with all of these instruction books, boxes, manuals, etc. Fill a plastic box with all the electronics warranties, purchase docs, and original boxes and slide it under the bed—organized, easy to access, and out of sight.

Hiding spots are ideal for items that we don't want or need out in the open. Thankfully, there are storage solutions specifically designed just for these kinds of spaces. Under the bed storage bins and bags as well as hanging shoe holders are low cost and highly effective. Under-bed storage is perfect for out of season clothing or bedding—close at hand when you need it but not taking up valuable closet and drawer space. Do you have young children with lots of Legos, Matchbox cars, or dolls? Use that under-bed space for small toy and doll storage. Bins on wheels are easy for them to pull out and use, and equally easy to gather up and store out of sight. Under the bed is the number one wasted storage space I see in my clients' homes.

So, what should I be "hiding"? Out of season clothing and

footwear, along with extra bedding, are great choices. In a child's room, toys *containerized* in shallow bins are stored perfectly under the bed. And this is a much better option than the usual stuff that gets shoved under there until it becomes a black hole of clutter. Containerizing is super important when you are using under-bed storage—it marks the difference between a storage system and a mess.

Another of my favorite organizing products is a clear, plastic shoe organizer. Install a clear plastic shoe hanger on the back of any door and fill it up!

In-season shoes are an obvious choice for a hanging shoe holder because this opens up floor space. I have seen many closets that are overflowing with shoes as well as the bulky shoe organizing units on the floor which takes up valuable space. Often clients don't bother using the shelving units at all and the shoes just jumble up on the closet floor. Getting these shoes up off the closet or bedroom floor is both a physical and visual plus.

While shoes are the obvious choice for these hanging pockets, there are so many ways to use this storage! As long as you have solid wooden doors, you can install them in almost any room in the home or office. Fill the clear shoe pockets with small toys, hair accessories, health and

Organizing Tip

Unless a client has a strong preference, I don't use the over the door clips that are included with these because I feel they are too flimsy. Instead I screw the shoe hanger into the door itself at the top and the bottom so it does not bump around when the door is opening and closing.

beauty items, dog care items, scarves—the possibilities are endless. In homes with pets, I recommend storing leashes, poo bags, grooming tools, and pet toys in the pockets. Hang this on a door near the exit and everything you need to take Fido for a walk is ready to go. On the back of a bathroom door, this works for small towels, health and beauty products, grooming tools, etc. By utilizing this storage, you move products from the counter tops and inside the shower to clearer, less cluttered space.

This storage solution can be used in the home and office and keeps horizontal surfaces clear and clutter free. Another plus of using clear shoe pockets is that you have a much better visual on your items. Try storing socks and tights in these, and open up your drawer space. Arts and craft supplies, colored pencils, and markers, glue, and stickers fit great so install one in your playroom. Clean up is easy and so is access. Are there items which are not for independent play? Reserve the top rows for items your child cannot access without adult help. Be creative. Think about how your space is used so you can create solutions that work for you.

In the kitchen or utility room, the shoe pocket organizer is a great option for anything that takes up counter or shelf space. For a transitional space, pockets hold gloves and mittens, small umbrellas, dog leashes, and bags—all those items we need every day. In an office, this storage solution holds stationery supplies, cleaning products, and personal items much more effectively than in a jumble in a drawer or closet. And don't limit this item to doors only. Screw the shoe pockets onto the wall behind the door and you really maximize your storage space.

Vertical wall space is one of the most underutilized spaces in any home or office. The backs of doors, unused wall space, blank spaces over desks or beds are ideal for additional storage. In addition to using hanging shoe pockets or additional shelving, there are other, easy options to use this underutilized space.

A simple butler's hook on the back of the door allows for more hanging space. This is perfect for hanging up bathrobes, pajamas, and loungewear. For a mere five dollars and five minutes of work, you have another place to hang something up instead of laying it down. I always recommend butler hooks or a rack of hooks if that will fit the space. This is the perfect spot to put out your outfit for the morning. By removing tomorrow's outfit from the closet and hanging it in a separate space—i.e. the butler's hook—you take stress out of getting dressed and getting out the door in the morning. You know you have an outfit ready to go and you can prep anything that still needs to be done, like ironing.

Floating shelves or wall shelving are more easy and versatile uses of vertical space. Using the vertical of open space is particularly good for display. In a child's room, floating shelves make a great display for trophies, photos, special trinkets—all those items that generally end up on the flat surfaces in the room. This same principle applies for adult space—in an office, master bedroom, living room, etc. Any time we can take things off of the horizontal surfaces, it makes it easier to see, enjoy, and these items don't get "lost" within the room.

While we can't really create space—it is finite—we can find optimal solutions to utilizing the space we have.

More Time

Seriously, who doesn't want more time? Pretty much everyone. But is all time the same? Do we value ourselves and others when we "waste time"? Time is a valuable commodity and we should all learn to use it more wisely.

11

How Does Being Organized Save Me Time?

"Time has a wonderful way of showing us what really matters."

—**Margaret Peters**

How much time do you waste looking for items that are misplaced and things you cannot find? Have you ever run around in the morning, trying to get out the door to work, while frantically looking for your keys or wallet? Have you ever been on a conference call, making dinner, and helping with homework while searching for the uniform your child needs *now* to get out the door to practice? Ever sat down to start on a work project and return calls when a colleague flew into your office needing help locating a missing report?

Does any of this sound familiar? The result of all this searching for "lost" items? Stress. Frustration. Recreating or repurchasing the missing item. Wasted money and *time*. How could you better use that time? Organizing isn't pretty boxes and bins and complicated organizing systems. It's finding your stuff when you need it so you can go out and live your best life. So, how can you make it different?

I've given many presentations over the years and I always query the participants on what their number one "lost" item is. What's the mystery item that never seems to be available when you need it? The top offenders in the "Where the heck is it?" category? Wallets, car keys, purses, and mobile phones. If you have those, along with your other items, organized so you weren't always searching frantically for them, how would that feel? That's the feeling that organizing can give you; knowing that you can put your hands on what you need when you need it. How do you create an organizing solution so that you don't waste that time again?

First, create a home for every item in your space. Yes, every item. This doesn't have to be complicated so don't overthink it. In our desire to create a perfect solution, we can really overcomplicate life and make things even harder for ourselves. My wallet, when not in my pocket, lives on my bedroom bureau. In the house, my purse hangs on a hook in the mudroom. I hang my car keys on the key rack in the mudroom when I enter the house. I carry my mobile phone in my pocket or it lives on the charging shelf in the kitchen. Important, critical documents are filed in my working files and my forever documents are housed securely in another space. By creating a routine and a system, we have a go-to spot for our things, resulting in much less lost time searching for misplaced items.

Let's take a minute and talk about our critical electronics and where they should "live" so that they actually work for us. Our culture is tech-centric. We all have multiple devices in use. In addition, there are the many discarded and unused tech items filling our homes and offices. For now, I'm focused on the current phones, tablets, laptops, and other mobile devices that are in use. Or are they? Just because we have all of these electronics hanging around, does that mean they are actually being used?

How often have you encountered this scenario? You need to use your laptop, cell phone, or tablet only to find that your daughter borrowed it and now you have to search her room to find it. Or your partner usually uses the tablet in the family room but it's not there when you go looking for it. When you eventually find the item, it needs to be charged. But you can't find the "right" charging cord because you can't remember where you used it last. Or you brought an extra cord into the office and you thought you put it in your desk. When you look in the jumble of your desk drawer, there's a mess of cords and chargers you have to sort through. This is wasted time! Wasted time when you are searching for the item, wasted time looking for the right charger, wasted time waiting for the item to charge so you can use it.

I recommend creating a dedicated "electronics space" in the home and office. This will save you more time than you can possibly imagine. It's that one space that houses all the electronics in use and their charging cords. At a certain age, your kids will keep their electronics in their own spaces and they will need to become responsible for keeping track of the electronics and the chargers. But when you have littles and want to let them use the tablet or laptop for games or homework, keep it in your electronics space. For most families, this area is generally located in the kitchen, the hub of the home. If you don't have the room for this in the kitchen, choose a nearby space.

During a renovation, I planned and created a special electronics shelf in my kitchen and had the electrician install an extra long multi-prong outlet especially for this. I keep my electronics in this space *at all times*. I know where everything is and the items are all fully charged (because the plugs and cords are there for charging). I know that I am prepared and organized for when I need my electronics. You don't need to reconstruct your space to achieve this. But be intentional. Think through how and where you will need your electronics and be consistent. You have control over this so

Organizing Tip

You can create the best organizing systems and solutions imaginable but you have to use and maintain them. If you bypass hanging up your keys when you enter, you'll end up searching all over when you, or someone else, needs those keys. If you don't return the laptop or cell phone to the charging station, it won't be there and ready to use when you need it. As Brian Tracy said so well, "Successful people are simply those with successful habits." It isn't enough to create a system; you have to *use* it.

make this work for you. This is one of the ways you find more time in your life—by not wasting the time you have.

Here's the reality of life and organizing: stuff happens. We're in a rush, we're distracted by our next task (my biggest challenge!), and we forget where we put something. Or we just can't find it, regardless of how great our organizing system is. Here's what I recommend to counter that: redundancy, redundancy, redundancy. While this is something that I recommend for backing up our e-life, it's also critical for other areas as well—call it a "life hack." Have you ever tried to walk out of the house only to find that your wallet or keys are not where they should be? Or you misplace your cell phone in the house and you can't call it because it's dead or on silent?

While I'm generally not a "product" person, I recently found a product that I recommend to everyone: Tile. This genius piece of technology can be a true lifesaver. If you want to spend less time looking for things and stressing out, and losing time and money in the process, try this product. There is a version you can add to your keychain (the Tile Mate), which makes it perfect for car keys, house keys, and dorm keys. The Tile Slim can slip into a wallet, purse, or adhere to many electronics. Once you download the Tile app to your smartphone, you can ring the Tile to find the missing item. If the cell phone is the item you've misplaced, you can use a computer or any other Tile to locate it. Out of earshot? The Tile will show up on a map, showing you exactly where the item is.

Organizing is anything that makes my life easier and run smoother with less stress and frustration. Losing keys or a wallet and scrambling around to find your missing item is stressful and time consuming. Creating a "home" for your items is a great Plan A and Tile is a great Plan B. We lose time—remember all those missing minutes each day? How much richer and more enjoyable would your life be with that "extra" time back? How much more joy would you have?

We all want more time. And regardless of what the Rolling Stones said, time doesn't always feel like it's on our side. When we store our stuff in its proper home, we don't have to go searching for it and wasting that time. That's a major, well, time saver. But another way we waste a lot of time is that we don't complete a project or task the first time we start it. We have to go back and finish or redo it again, thereby wasting time. In organizing, we call it the "touch it twice" rule. In essence, it means that you touch an item or project only twice—do it and be done. Complete a task right away or deal with the email or paperwork and then put it away. By doing this, you eliminate the need to go back and complete the task at another point. Don't "touch it" more than twice and elongate the process.

In addition to making your life simpler and easier, there's real science behind this concept. In physics, it's called activation energy, or the activation rate. Simply put, it's the amount of energy you need to start or activate a reaction or in this case, start a task. Once started however, the acceleration rate is much greater. So what does this mean for your organizing process? It means that once you get over the hurdle of starting a task or project, no matter how big or small, the amount of energy it takes to complete it is much lower. This is why I encourage the "touch it twice" rule. It's when we start and stop and then start again that we need so much more time and energy to get organized. Momentum is critical in organizing.

Here's the thing about real life. You won't always have enough time to complete a more complicated and time consuming task. You will have to "touch" that task more than twice to get it done. Organizing a large space like a garage or basement are good examples. Or creating an effective filing system, or completing your taxes. So, how do you make sure the task does get done? Put it on the "to-do list" and plan an appropriate length of time to complete the project. For simpler tasks, do it and be done. Don't let groceries sit out waiting to be put away—put them away immediately. Don't pick up the pile of mail and then put it down again, untouched. Process it and move on. You will only have to touch it twice and not move the items around continually.

Be proactive and consistent about making decisions and taking action so that clutter doesn't build. Implementing the "touch it twice" rule is really effective for this. Clutter is deferred decisions. I pick up an item and I don't know

Organizing Tip

Organizing is a process, not an event. The "touch it twice" rule applies to particular tasks, some as simple as returning the hammer to its spot in the garage or plugging the laptop back into the charging station. Organizing as a process means breaking down the overall project into manageable chunks and completing those individual tasks.

what to do with it. Should I keep it? Why am I keeping it? Where should I keep it? I don't make a decision so I put it down and it becomes clutter. Decide to decide. The "touch it twice" rule can be applied to multiple tasks in your home and office: laundry, mail and paperwork sorting, toy organization, closet and wardrobe, etc. Choose an item, complete the task associated with the item and then either put it away or purge it. Don't pick it up, move it to a new spot, half complete the task and then have to start the task again at another time. Touch it twice and be done with it.

Along with deferred decisions, the enemy of organization and efficiency is perfection. We look at social media, TV, and magazines and we think we're not doing it as well as everyone else and we are failing. We see party ideas on Pinterest and believe we are falling short because we aren't creating the "perfect" event. You are enough. You don't need to compete with anyone. Let go of the notion that you have to do everything "perfectly" because that is self-defeating, negative, and unrealistic. Doing laundry, putting away groceries, picking a gift, making a meal, completing most projects—this is when good enough really is good enough. Every meal is not going to be a four course masterpiece; every wall paint color is not going to be show-home worthy. The point is that we understand when good enough really is good enough and perfection is not necessary. We waste so much time dithering about the small details and trying to achieve "perfection." In the end, we get caught in the weeds and end up completing nothing because of our "analysis paralysis." Time is a valuable commodity and we should spend it wisely.

We waste time trying to make the best, the perfect, and the optimal choice. Because of this, we defer doing anything. Focus on doing some things really well—parenting, relationships, health and wellness, your work, finances—that's where it's important. For most tasks, doing it and being done is good enough. This is the way to get organized and find more time.

12

Prioritizing Time

"Lost time is never found again."

—Benjamin Franklin

s an organizing coach, I help my clients move from feeling frazzled and overwhelmed to living a less stressed, more intentional life. To be organized and find more space, more time, and more joy, respecting your time is key. In business and life, there's a lot of talk about "time management." In my work, and in my life, I've found that managing time is a false concept. We think of time as finite; sixty minutes in an hour, twenty-four hours in a day, seven days in a week. In this model, all time is "equal" and definitive. But have you ever sat in a meeting or class, agonizingly watching the clock and waiting for it to be over? Did it feel like "time stood still"? Have you watched an incident or accident unfold and it felt like time slowed down?

Conversely, when we are in a happy or pleasurable situation, it feels like time speeds up or is "flying by" when we are happily engaged. We have so many references to time in our life: "fighting against the clock," or trying to "beat the clock." We can't manage or defeat time but we can prioritize it.

My focus, and what I coach my clients on, is better management of our priorities and tasks. Setting priorities is the basis of living an intentional life. Where and how will I spend my time? On my work, on my fitness and wellness, on my relationships? Or on passive activities like social media and watching TV? That's time prioritization. There are lots of tools for better time prioritization like calendar systems, timers, and "smart" electronics. Is your goal to stop running around like a chicken with its head cut off, scrambling from one crisis to another? First determine, "What's the real value of my time?"

Most of us don't know the true value of our time so we waste it on unnecessary tasks that consume too much time, effort, and resources. We spend our days running around, feeling stressed and overwhelmed, "fighting fires" all the time. This is reactive behavior; we are reacting to events and mismanaging our time. Yes, of course there will always be emergencies and tasks and events that we have to address immediately—that's real life. But this should not be the norm; this should be the exception. In our hyper-driven society, we have become adrenaline junkies "needing" to jump into crisis mode. What is that about? Is it a diversion tactic? Is our everyday life so boring that we create and elevate crises so that we can feel justified and valued? Marianne Williamson, the American author, lecturer, entrepreneur, and activist, reminds us that we bring a particular energy to a situation: "Everything we do is infused with the energy in which we do it. If we're frantic, life will be frantic. If we are peaceful, life will be peaceful."

How do I start to move out of this frantic mode? Be more intentional with your time and your choices. Planning your time is an effective strategy for being organized. Break down a "typical" day into time blocks: morning, work/school, after school/work, evening, etc. Within those segments, pinpoint the tasks that you need to complete in each block. Focus on tasks that must get done at a certain time. Getting in a workout, making breakfast, readying kids for school—those are all time-sensitive tasks that must be done in the morning. Don't use that time to focus on other tasks that can wait. If everyone must get out the door to work and school by 7:30 a.m., the early morning routine needs to be streamlined to make that happen with as little distraction and frustration as possible.

Outline and define your "time chunks." This planning is critical! All successful companies and businesses delineate tasks and responsibilities and create a time line for completing projects. Can you bring some of that business planning to your

Organizing Tip

The morning rush time is not the time to start another task or project that can wait. Are you in the habit of checking email and social media first thing in the morning and then getting distracted? Once distracted, we lose time and the result is rushing around, feeling stressed.

daily routines? The idea is not to become rigid and business-like; the goal is to remove chaos and stress because we have no plan on how to move through the day. Space and time are finite; we have to bring flexibility and some creativity into how to best use it to our advantage.

In a given time frame or time block, what tasks can you do best? Are you maximizing your time and effort or can you tweak your system for improvement? When my sons entered high school and they had to be at school by 7:30 a.m. I altered my routine and it made a significant difference for all of us. While I have always been a morning person (a lark, if you will), I created a new habit of getting up at 5:00 a.m. during the school week. This was not an easy habit to create! But by getting up earlier, I was ready for work *before* my kids got up. Once they were up, I could focus exclusively on getting them out the door for school. This change made a huge impact on my mornings.

> **Caveat: You don't need to get up at the crack of dawn to be effective in your day. My "night owl" friends shudder at the idea of getting up so early so that doesn't work for them. Figure out what you need to do to make your routine work for you.**

In life, we all have a skill set that makes us effective and productive. Conversely, we all muddle through some tasks that we could outsource to make the balance of our time more productive and less stressed. Do you like to cook but hate to grocery shop? Transition grocery shopping to another family member or use one of the many grocery delivery services available (hello, Peapod). Do you love Fido but getting in a long walk just doesn't fit in your schedule most mornings? Give that task to a household member with more time and flexibility. Also, some folks spend their days walking dogs! Hire a professional dog walker or find a neighbor to hire or, even better, barter services with. Know that there is someone, some-where, who will gladly take over the tasks that don't fit in your schedule or skill set.

Organizing Tip

Work to your strength and hire to your weakness. Welcome to the new service economy!

What would you define as your greatest pain point or time challenge? Your pain point is that challenge that's causing you the most stress and frustration. This is what is likely impeding your ability to get organized. This "pain point" can result from either a poor use of space or a time chal-lenge. Go back to the time blocks/chunks to narrow down where the greatest challenges arise. Is it when everyone enters the kitchen in the morning? Are there lots of bodies milling around getting in each others' way trying to figure out breakfast? Do you have a designated breakfast space and routine? If not, plan one to eliminate that chaos.

The enemies of organization are perfection and lack of plan-ning. It's Tuesday morning, it's snowing, and you have to drive your fifth grader to school with her science project. Today is not the day for a four course breakfast or elaborate hair styling. I see many clients put up roadblocks to success by trying to be the "perfect parent" or create the "perfect moment" or memory. Plan the night before to get up a few minutes early, put out cereal for breakfast and agree on the outfit for the next day. Stop engaging in self-defeating habits and behaviors. By planning your day the night before, you can figure out where the snafus might occur and be prepared. *The Lion King* was a big hit in our house. It came out when my boys were young and we watched that movie countless times. So my catch phrase became: "Be prepared!" Thanks, Scar.

Did you decide that your morning bottleneck occurs before everyone gets to a common space? Wardrobe or closet disorganization is the likely culprit. Closets and drawers that are overstuffed with clothes that don't fit or don't look great will set you up for frustration every single time. I believe that what we wear should make us look and feel good and I live by that mantra. This is so important that I will devote a chapter to it in the next section. Again, this is where planning makes all the difference. Plan what you'll wear the next day prior to standing in front of the closet at 7:00 a.m. and staring at it blankly. Save spontaneity for other areas of your life—this is not it. Frustration is not the tone you want to set for the day.

Once everyone's dressed and eaten, can you "grab and go" to get out the door? Are backpacks, athletic bags, and work bags in a designated spot and at the ready? This is where dedicated transitional space becomes absolutely critical to get everyone out the door quickly. I urge you to plan out your daily time line. Once you focus on this, you can really see where our space management—transitional space, wardrobe, kitchen set-up—needs to be better organized or tweaked. Most of the time, this will align very closely with your pain point or time challenge. These are so intertwined that you can't address one without defining or understanding the other. I love Gretchen Rubin's quote from her "Here's My Habits Manifesto. What's Yours?" She says, "We're not very different from other people, but those differences are very important." Determine *your* pain points and address them. Don't waste time and energy creating elaborate and complex systems. No one needs to be creative before 8:00 a.m., and it's okay to have the same routine most days.

Remember how we spend all that time looking for something we've lost? Well, sometimes what we can't locate isn't something physical; it's information. There are some pieces of information in the home that are critical to be able to access in a hurry, especially when it relates to safety and repairs. You open the freezer for an icepack for your child's lunch and the ice cream is pooling on the bottom shelf. Can you put your hands on the manual and receipt for your non-working refrigerator in less than five minutes? Found the manual? Great. Is it still under warranty and when and where did I purchase this anyway?

Organization is finding my stuff when I need it. Information, especially information on items we've purchased, is critical to be able to put our hands on immediately. I recommend using an alpha file for organizing most purchase information. When you buy a new item (appliance, furniture, pricey clothing item), place the manual with the attached receipt in the alpha file. I house my alpha file in a drawer in my armoire so that it is readily available but not taking up "prime real estate." I highly recommend an alpha file as opposed to putting these receipts and manuals in Pendaflex files in your filing cabinet. These documents are often bulky

Organizing Tip

As an added step in organizing your product information, write on the front of the manual the purchase place and date for easy reference and staple the original receipt to it. Most manuals and product information can be downloaded as a PDF if you prefer. But I do recommend holding onto the original receipt. Yes, lots of folks like to keep these receipts in email format but a hard copy is always easier to retrieve in a hurry.

and can take up a lot of space. (Remove the foreign language portion of the manual to get rid of the bulk. It's unlikely you're going to be looking up replacement parts in Spanish. And if you are, good for you!)

When you purchase a replacement item—like a new washing machine or new iPhone—be sure to discard the old manual! In your electronics box, mark product boxes and receipts with simple notes: "Lisa's iPhone6 purchased Sept 2017." When you need to have an item repaired, you don't need to be searching through a pile of manuals and receipts for the right one. How much time will you gain back if you can eliminate these seek and find missions?

13

How Do I Prioritize My Time with Better Systems?

"Time is what we want most but what we use worst."

—William Penn

Organization is about finding our stuff when we need it so we can have more space, more time, and more joy in our lives. Can I manage or organize time? Technically, yes. You can create a schedule and hope that events and timing cooperate. "How's that working out for ya?" as Dr. Phil would ask. Even the best plans don't always work out because "stuff" keeps popping up in our day and throwing our schedule off track. Does that mean we just let go of planning our time and allow chaos to ensue? Ahhh … no. Instead, *prioritize* your time.

Decide what's really worth your time and effort. Focus on tasks that are going to have maximum impact. Some days that means doubling down on a work project. Another time it's spending the day with friends or cuddling with your sick toddler. Life is about balance. At certain points in the year, your focus and time will be spent on preparing for holidays and celebrations. Peter Drucker put it a little differently but the end result is the same: "Until we can manage time, we can manage nothing else." While I choose the word *prioritize* over *manage*, it's the same difference. It's when we don't set priorities and have intention in our lives that we make reactive, not proactive, choices. In that mode, we allow circumstances and other peoples' priorities to run our lives. Consistently I have seen this lead to stress, frustration, and the proverbial "running around like a chicken without a head." Is that how you want to live?

One of the biggest time wasters that I work on with clients is mail: both physical mail and email. The amount of mail that arrives in our mailbox weekly is staggering. So much paper! Processing mail is a big challenge for a number of clients I've worked with over the years. The volume of it seems so overwhelming that we choose not to deal with it. Or we're afraid of what our bank statement or investment account looks like so we choose to ignore it. We put it in a pile, or a basket, or a drawer, and tell ourselves "I'll get to it soon." Do you know what else is growing along with that stack of mail? Anxiety. Stress. Indecision. This is a great example of

Organizing Tip

My practice is to process the mail as soon as it enters my space while standing over the paper recycling bin. Some clients like to gather the daily mail in a spot and deal with it all at once at the end of the week. If this is your process, great, go with it. But I strongly recommend processing the mail *at least once a week.* Time sensitive information will be missed if you allow it to go longer than a few days.

where creating a system makes all the difference. Step one: open the envelope!

There are only three kinds of mail or paperwork that enter your space: things you can discard immediately (junk mail), paperwork to file (like health insurance and bank statements) and actionable items (paperwork you have to act on). By far, the most common is junk mail. This is also the easiest to process because you just don't need to keep it. I immediately recycle junk mail and fliers, which account for 75 percent of the pile. With all mail, I recommend you open every envelope to be sure you know what's in it. I've seen clients throw out unopened mail, believing it is just a statement or so out-of-date that it is no longer relevant. You do you. But why are you getting statements in the mail if you don't open and read them? Go paperless and save yourself the time on processing those documents and be a little bit greener at the same time.

Junk mail, by its very nature, should be considered, well ... junk. Move quickly through this task but again, be intentional and focused. If you prefer to process your mail in chunks, sit down with a cup of coffee or tea and work through it. This task is a lot less daunting when we do it consistently and don't let the pile of mail get out of hand.

After junk mail, the second largest category of mail is generally paperwork to be filed. This category is pretty broad and can include bank and investment statements, insurance documents, and "hard copies" of bills we pay online. Again, if you are paying your bill or reviewing your statement online, why do you need a paper copy? When I ask clients this question, the response is often "I want to be able to look back and see what I paid/was charged last month" or "I like having a record of my expenses." If you have online access to your account, you already have these options available to you—you don't need a paper copy to get that historical data. Depending on your comfort level and tech savvy, online bill paying and account management is the way to go. It provides you current, to the day, accounting that a monthly bill or statement will not. Also, by going paperless, you will cut down on the volume of mail entering your space.

> **Caveat: For insurance policies, like auto, homeowners, and life insurance, it is critical to have the most recent and up to date policy available in hard copy. Be sure to file these documents as soon as possible so they are readily available.**

Actionable items, mail that we have to act on, is generally the smallest category of mail that we receive. A common actionable item is an invitation or upcoming event we need to respond to. Again, I believe we need to be intentional about our time. Review your calendar and talk with your partner (personal and business) before responding and adding it to your calendar.

If the invitation or event requires an additional step, like purchasing a gift or sending a payment, can you do that right now? Instead of deferring actions and saying "I'll get to that," just do it now if at all possible. Remember the "touch it twice" rule? Here's a great place to put it into action. So many options exist online for purchasing—is there a registry available for the wedding or baby shower? Or how about a gift certificate? Do not overcomplicate your life and waste precious time by spending countless hours searching for the "perfect" gift. Perfection is the enemy of organization. If the new parents or bride and groom have already registered with online retailers, don't recreate the wheel.

Do you receive a lot of magazines and periodicals in the mail? Choose a spot for your reading materials and place them there immediately. If you find that you don't have time to read these on a regular basis, cancel the subscription or

Organizing Tip

Create a space in your home or office to put all of these actionable items until you are ready to process them. An inbox, basket, or drawer all serve the same purpose: to safely contain the items you need to act on. Create time in your schedule to focus on these actionable items so you can complete them in the most efficient manner. Unless an item is critically time sensitive, don't stop everything else you're doing to complete it.

transfer it to a school or organization that could benefit from that resource. If you are consistently recycling unread publications, take a few minutes to redirect them.

If you are paying your bills online, you will only be responsible for processing infrequent bills and payments that come in the mail. Setting up auto-pay for monthly expenses like insurance, cable and phone, utilities, and other scheduled charges makes your life more organized and your time more efficient. Not everyone is comfortable with paying bills online and that's okay too. Just figure out your best system.

Along with invitations, another time-consuming actionable item we often receive is paperwork that needs to be completed. This paperwork comes from school, sports, recreation, activities, business—so much paperwork! Thankfully, a lot of documentation and paperwork has been moved online for sign ups, etc., but there is still a lot that has to be completed by hand, signed, and returned. I see a lot of clients, especially those with young children, overwhelmed by all this paperwork—especially at the start of a new school year or sports season. Schedule uninterrupted time for this project so you can get it done in an efficient manner. This is a task best left until after little ones are in bed or before they wake up in the morning. When my boys were school age, I often took paperwork with me when I knew I was going to be waiting—like at a doctor's appointment or waiting for after-school pick up. That's a way to use that downtime efficiently with "busy work" and double your effectiveness. Scrolling through social media while you are waiting is wasting precious time; take a few minutes to do some restorative deep breathing and then use the time wisely.

Whatever you choose as your system—either processing your mail daily or weekly—choose a process! I have worked with clients with years of unopened mail. When we don't address the mail, we are allowing fear to hold us back. Fear of what's in the statement. Fear of the test results in the doctor's letter. Fear of "knowing" because we're more comfortable with not knowing; all of this keeps us from opening the envelope. So we don't know what the reality is that we need to address. So we worry more. And we remain in an indecisive, negative spiral. Robert Frost said: "The only way around is through." By acknowledging and dealing with what is, we are better prepared and better organized.

Have you processed all the mail stacked up in your space? Congratulations. You've taken a huge step forward into better organization. Now, how about that inbox? In this day and age, who doesn't have an overloaded inbox? With all these incoming messages, it's very easy to get overloaded.

Like managing your physical mail, you have to take steps to declutter your inbox. I have seen clients with hundreds of emails sitting in their inbox and the clients swear it works for them. They are reluctant to move or delete anything for fear of it disappearing into the ether. What's your level of risk aversion? If you're sure the department email, once moved or deleted, can never be retrieved, keep it in your inbox. Create and follow the system that works for you. Organizing isn't about following my system; it's intuitive *to* you.

Caveat: Let me take a minute and talk about redundancy and backing up your data. I cannot emphasize *enough* **how important this is. For a business, redundancy and backing up data is a given but it's equally important for your personal data (which often includes photos). I have had clients with thousands of photos on their phones and this is not recommended! If you are not backing up to the cloud, choose a local backup. Cloud backup is inexpensive and easy to set up and I urge redundancy, redundancy, redundancy. Get on this. Now.**

I do recommend processing emails in a similar manner to processing your physical mail. First, eliminate the junk mail. Unsubscribe to email lists you signed up for with good intentions but that's not getting the information read. Unsubscribe if you know you can't prioritize reading this. The information exists on the web; you can always search for it in the future. You don't need to be constantly bombarded with emails when that's not your focus.

Organizing Tip

Don't just delete junk emails; unsubscribe and stop unwanted and unneeded emails from arriving in the first place and cluttering up your inbox. Yes, it's quicker just to delete, but if you scroll to the bottom of those pesky marketing emails, you'll see the "unsubscribe" button. Yes, you may have to do this more than once, but the space and time you open up in your inbox is priceless.

Now let's focus on filing away information you may really need to refer to at some point. Like with physical mail, you may need to hold onto this information but you don't need to act on it now. Create folders so you can file away emails to quickly find them in the future. Is the email related to Suzy's soccer? Just drag anything into the folder related to that subject. I create folders by year for Travel, Sports, Holidays, etc. I just drag anything that comes in into its appropriate file; organized and out of the inbox. You can always go back and reference the information when you need it.

Another easy organizing tip for emails is to create a "filter." Create a folder for certain emails to be downloaded to as opposed to it appearing in your inbox. Want anything related to shopping to go into a particular folder? Create a filter so it doesn't clutter your inbox and your really important emails don't get lost. Spend some time on setting up this system. Yes, I know that taking the time upfront to create the system seems cumbersome. We believe it's so much easier to just delete unwanted and unneeded emails and leave the remainder sitting in the inbox. I understand that the intention is to save time and effort, but as I love to say, "The road to hell is paved with good intentions." Do the work upfront; put in the planning and effort. The rewards and benefits of being organized are worth it.

What's the best way to handle emails that you need to act on or respond to? These are the ones to leave in your inbox. It's those few emails that are the visual reminder that I have to complete a task or follow up. Responding to some emails is easy, with a yes or no answer. "Yes, I can attend that meeting," or "No, I don't have an extra bundt pan to lend you." But real life is often more complicated than that. Before I respond to my colleague about the data analysis, I have to first complete the analysis and this takes time. For the most part, unless it is truly time sensitive, I employ the same methodology as I do with my actionable mail. Set aside the request until I have the time to process and complete the project efficiently and effectively. Email has become a huge time suck in our personal and business lives. Do not let other peoples' priorities become your priorities. Turn off your email notifications when you need to focus on a project so you aren't distracted by the constant interruptions.

Like any system, you have to maintain and tweak your email processes. Delete unneeded file folders. Did you create an email file folder for Sam's fourth grade class? Great. But now he's heading to high school so it's time to delete that folder.

Organizing Tip

I'm calling this an "Organizing Tip" but you can also file this under "Lisa's Pet Peeves." Do not "reply all" unless absolutely necessary! If the email asks for volunteers to bring snacks to the upcoming game, responding all is appropriate. "I'll bring oranges for half-time," is an appropriate response so the process is organized. Well done. "Thanks, Bob!" is not an appropriate response to the thirty people on the work email when Bob informs everyone that tomorrow's meeting is now in the large conference room. Stop wasting time, yours and everyone else's. Get organized and use email appropriately.

It's not enough to create an organizing system and then assume that it will remain useful ad infinitum. Organizing systems, designed to make our lives easier, need to be adaptive as our needs change. Don't create overly complicated rules and systems for your mail, physical and email. Be mindful about updating your system as circumstances change.

Another way to organize and prioritize your time optimally is to invest in an effective calendar system. There are so many options available so sometimes this can take a few tries before you find the one that works best for you. Spend some time at the office supply or stationery store checking out your options if you are looking for a physical system. Or ask for recommendations from folks who love an online calendar—Cosi is a popular choice. Then commit to using the calendar system that works best for you. It is virtually impossible to effectively prioritize your time—and your productivity—if you do not have a handle on your schedule. A calendar system, when used effectively, can help you better manage your schedule so you are not wasting time and money. Time is a precious commodity; don't waste it.

Today there are many, many options for calendar systems. I use a spiral calendar system that I carry with me. It has a monthly and weekly view for eighteen months. This type of planning gives me flexibility to book appointments, events, and commitments with both long-term and hourly precision. The downfall? If I lose my calendar—which I do refer to as "The Bible"—this information will be truly lost. In almost two decades of using this, I have never, thankfully, lost it. I use the MOMAgenda products (you can check out their products online), which is similar to a DayTimer system. It is substantially sized and I invested in a quality, leather cover in a lovely medium blue so it is easy to spot in my bag and hard to lose. Fingers crossed....

Electronic calendars are a great option for people who prefer to store this information on their phone, desktop, or in the cloud. One of the advantages is that this information can be easily shared with others to coordinate schedules. While this does come with some ease of use and flexibility, there are downsides. Firstly, if the technology is unavailable—no internet or the server is down—you are unable to access the information when you need it. Secondly, when information is online and in the cloud, there is always the possibility of it being hacked.

And yes, I am aware that there is a calendar on my smartphone! While I love this feature and being able to quickly access this information, I don't use it for my overall calendar system and here's why: When you pull up the calendar function on your phone, booking an appointment on October 3rd looks great. What that limited view might not reflect is significant commitments before and after that date. I recommend a "wider view" of your overall schedule. It's this type of long-range planning that helps take the stress and overwhelm out of our schedule.

Organizing Tip

Again, this is a personal choice to use a paper-based system or a technology-based system. Play around with it and be flexible. Maybe a combination is an effective choice for you. Any system is better than no system at all.

14

Tackling
Techno-Clutter

*"Simple can be harder than complex. You
have to work hard to get your thinking clean
to make it simple."*

—**Steve Jobs**

Think back to when you were a child and there was one rotary phone, maybe two, in your entire home. I remember when my mother got a super-long cord so she could walk around the kitchen getting things done while she talked on the phone on the wall. That seemed revolutionary at the time. Now toddlers use electronics and grade schoolers own smartphones. Today, you can run a multinational business with a smartphone, Bluetooth, and Wi-Fi from a coffee shop. The speed of technology has increased dramatically in just a few years. Have your organizational systems kept up with the pace of technological change?

I've often done Facebook Live segments and asked my followers for common organizing challenges to address. One of my favorites, and one of the most common situations, was offered by a friend in Dallas. Her question was, "What do I do with all those old cords and chargers stuffed in drawers and baskets all over my house?" In our modern homes and offices, many of us have gone through a generation or two of technology—and that's in the last few years alone. As a result, we've upgraded our tablets, computers, and phones so many times that we are left with a graveyard of retired technology and a jumble of cords and wires we can't identify and are terrified to throw out "just in case." In clients' offices, I've seen entire closets and cabinets filled with old electronics and phone systems just sitting there and taking up space, both physical and psychological.

Have you ever picked up a cord or charger and thought, "What the heck is this for?" Ever spent time searching for the charging cord for your current phone and get frustrated by the inability to complete that "simple" task? What do you do when you open a drawer and find it jammed with cords and chargers and electronics you haven't used in months or years? Do you quickly close the drawer and hope it all just goes away because you feel so overwhelmed by it? Stop. You are deferring decisions and wasting valuable storage space with techno-clutter. So what's a good first step to organizing your technology jumble?

Start by labeling your current technology chargers and cables. Using a label maker or masking tape, create a sticky label for the cord. Use simple names like "Lisa's iPhone," "Conor's Kindle," "Brett's MAC"—you get the idea. Don't be afraid to over tag—it's better to have more tags than not. Because my son's laptop was the same as mine, the cords got a label. Once, he had his laptop plugged in for class but when he packed up, he forgot to grab the cord. Luckily for him, his girlfriend had a class right after in the same room. She knew that the cord, labeled "Conor's laptop" was his and promptly returned it to him. Fifteen seconds with a label maker saved a lot of time, hassle, and money.

As an added step to managing and organizing your technology tangle, create a "technology box." I recommend a plastic, shoe box-size bin with a cover to keep these small items contained. Put an elastic around the spare cables to keep them from getting tangled and put them in a small zip top bag. On the bag, write the phone these go to so there is no guessing when you need them. Do the same with plugs and extra headphones. I store a "travel technology kit" here along with my other technology extras because I need it frequently. I have a double wall plug, two USB charging

Organizing Tip

This is one category that I recommend "over-purchasing." When I get down to the last set of earbuds or charging cord for the current smartphone series, I purchase in bulk. We always need extras in our house as we all have the same phones. Finding that one of my kids has taken my charging cord because he left his at school is a real annoyance. I purchase mine in bulk on eBay or Amazon so we never run out and have to pay retail.

cables, and my portable power in the travel kit. When I'm heading out of town, even for an overnight, I just "grab and go" with my travel kit. No pulling cables out of the wall and then having to set it all back up when I return. Instead, I just put my travel kit away until my next trip.

For our family, I chose a shelf in the dining room sideboard to store our extra tech accessories because it was the best choice for us. It's central and accessible to all of us and everyone knows where to go when they need new earbuds or a charging cord. Pick the spot that works for your home or company. A drawer in the home office, a spot in the kitchen, a shelf in the central supply closet—pick your best spot. Some clients I've worked with prefer to keep their technology travel kits with their luggage. If that works for you, great. For me, it's intuitive to find all my technology together—in the technology box. Not only do I know where to find it but it is also readily accessible to everyone else in my home. No more, "Mom, I need new headphones!" or "Mom, my charging cord isn't working anymore." I keep the box in one spot in the house and everyone knows where to find it. This works well in an office too as it eliminates the hunt for an extra charging cord or power strip when needed.

Now, what about the "old" technology and mystery cords lurking in desks, drawers, and baskets all over the house? Step one: gather all the cords, chargers, techno-stuff together. Be sure to check kids' rooms too—technology will migrate there as your kids get older. Don't forget all the learning and educational toys your child once used. The LeapFrogs, learning tablets, and the like might not be in

Organizing Tip

In addition to a technology box, I also recommend a "battery box." Choose a sturdy plastic bin with a cover. For the home, a shoe box-size bin should work and for the office, something slightly larger. Put all batteries into the container. This eliminates rushing around trying to find replacements when the TV clicker stops working. Again, store this container in a central spot in your space so everyone can be responsible for changing the batteries as needed.

current use but are likely still hanging around and the cords might be separated from the device.

Then one by one, try to figure out which device the cord goes with. Give yourself some time to complete this project. You've spent years accumulating all of this technology so this project can't be done in fifteen minutes. Plan sixty to ninety minutes to figure out what goes with what. Hint: check the battery plug. The plug will often have the manufacturer's name on it. Do your best to figure out what goes with what but don't obsess. If you haven't missed it recently, it's unlikely you'll miss it in the future. Worst case scenario, you can always buy a replacement cord or charger online in twenty-four hours for most anything. How did we ever live without Amazon Prime?

Did you find the LeapPad and corresponding charging cord? Excellent detective work! Put the electronics and the charger—along with any corresponding pieces—into a large zip top bag so everything is contained. If your child has outgrown this educational toy, figure out right now what to do with it. Is there a neighbor or family member who could use this? Is there a tag sale coming up at your synagogue or church you can donate this to? Donate and move this item on today so that someone, somewhere is using it.

> **Caveat: If you plan on selling this item, be sure that it is complete or state that you are selling "as is." Local Facebook Marketplace sites are a great place to sell this kind of item. Be realistic about how much it's worth—check eBay for a comparison. Know that moving this item out of your space brings the most value and a little bit of cash is a bonus.**

At the end of your sorting session, I guarantee you will still be left with some unidentifiable items. Don't throw those unneeded and mystery cords and chargers in the trash—techno-trash is a real problem. Take them to Best Buy or Staples and drop them off for proper recycling. "Green" recycling of technology is really important because it concerns safety, both for the environment and for your financial well-being.

In my work, I have seen many "technology graveyards." While the scale varies, most homes and offices have at least one or two old computers and phones lying around or stuffed away in a closet or cabinet, taking up space. Recycling of cell phones is easier to manage so let's start here. If your provider won't buy it back, try reselling your "slightly" older model online. My husband's company discontinued using Blackberries (yup, that was a thing), and I sold them all online, netting almost $100 each. Again, this is a great place to use Facebook Marketplace or eBay. Some folks are eager to buy your last generation phone to upgrade theirs or replace a broken one. If you prefer not to spend time on trying to sell your phone, there are many great organizations that will gladly take this item off your hands. These phones are repurposed for military members, seniors, and the homeless.

Regardless of the option you choose, be sure to remove any personal data from your phone before moving it on. Resetting the phone to factory settings will remove any historical and personal information on the phone. You can find instructions online on how to complete this task if you don't have the instruction manual. Once you've wiped the phone clean, seal it in the zip top bag with all its cords and chargers and get it gone from your space.

One of my first clients was a technology entrepreneur who built a hugely successful business. One of the results of this growth was continuing expansion into new space as the company's operations grew and expanded. This was great! However, one of the negatives was that with the continued growth, the old technology was uninstalled and stacked away because they were focused on the new technology. So they had rooms and rooms stacked with slightly older tech equipment that was no longer being used that might have been resold and repurposed. When it comes to technology, as well as with most other things we purchase, that item is losing its value almost immediately after we purchase it. According to CARFAX, a new car loses 10% of its value in the first month![5] With the rapid pace of technology and electronics today, this is even truer. If you intend to sell your "older" model when you replace it, do it as soon as possible. The longer you wait, the more the price and value will drop. Yes, there are classic cars and timeless and vintage couture, but for technology, your greatest bang for your buck comes sooner than later.

As with cell phones, it is imperative to remove any personal data from your tablet and computer when you are done with it. Once you've bridged any pertinent data and you feel comfortable that your new system is up and running well, deal with the old technology. Spend the money on an IT professional to wipe or remove the hard drive on computers—this is your personal and financial information and your security is priceless. Resell the technology if possible or donate or recycle.

I have a great IT guy who has been amazing to work with over the years. I give him my clients' old technology and he wipes the hard drives. He then repurposes the technology by donating it to Learn to Read programs for adults learning English as a second language. These simple programs work perfectly on older and slower computers that would otherwise be cluttering up your space. This is a perfect example of living an intentional life. Make a decision about what to do with X and then execute on it. Don't defer the decision and let that item sit, unused and unneeded. Don't become so focused on the *next* thing in your life that you neglect to deal effectively with what you already have. Shoving something into the closet, or basement, or attic to be dealt with at some nebulous point in the future is not intentional. Intention requires both strategic and peripheral vision. For your business, reselling hardware could be a great way to offset new capital purchases and technology investments. Designate someone, perhaps within the IT department, to be responsible for reselling technology. Or consider donating all of your unused technology for the tax benefit. Just because you have room to store something doesn't mean that you should.

In our business and in our life, we start out with a plan (sometimes, anyway...). And for a while, the technology and systems we chose work for us until they don't. It's what we do from there that drives an intentional and organized mindset or not. This is true not just with the products we use but also with the systems we create. Recognizing that things aren't working optimally anymore is important. Having our "unused and unneeded" in the closet or basement is similar to ignoring that a system we've created isn't a good solution any longer. We're going to have a lot of technology and electronics in our space; that's a given of our modern culture. How we manage and organize those items is important. It can mean the difference between finding what you need when you need it or wasting time searching for missing and misplaced things. It's the difference between an intentional and mindful life or a stressed and overwhelmed state. Which do you choose?

15

Are You Keeping Pace with Change?

"Things that matter the most must never be at the mercy of things which matter least."

—Goethe

*T*ime is a funny thing. We think of time as finite; with clear, measurable intervals that define and drive our lives. School starts at 8:00 a.m. I have to be in the office by nine. Conference call at 1:00 p.m. with the new vendor. Soccer practice at 4:30 p.m. and parent-teacher conference at 7:30 p.m. But the funny thing about time is that it isn't always linear in the way we experience it. Think back to when you were a little kid playing outside in the summer. Did the summer seem to stretch out endlessly before you? What parent hasn't blinked and it's already time for the "newborn's" first birthday? We enter high school and graduation seems so far away; but then it's over and we wonder where the time went.

That's the reality of time as we experience it. It can seem fast or slow depending on the framework we're in. Ever sat with a friend waiting for test results from the biopsy? Waited for a call from someone you love? Time seems to slow to a crawl. But it's the same amount of time; we just experience it differently. Every year since my boys were little, we've camped for a weekend each summer with friends. When we're camping, time spent there both slows down and speeds up. Because we're spending time with people we love, apart from our "real" lives, those days seem different somehow. That moment and space in time, repeated year after year, stands apart and still; always there to come back to. Why does that feel so different from the seventy-two hours we spent last weekend?

Time really is flexible and expansive and we need to be more receptive and adaptive to that notion. What worked yesterday doesn't always work today. The communication you had with a new hire yesterday is not going to motivate a seasoned employee. The rules you set up for your grade schooler will absolutely not work with your high schooler. The way I ate and worked out ten years ago is not going to keep me healthy and fit as I age now. The model is changing; are you?

In working with clients, I've learned that sometimes it's our fidelity and adherence to the stories we give the situations in our lives that can hold us back from making the changes we need to make.

"I created this filing system just a few years ago (almost 10!) so it's still a good system."

"We've invested a lot of time and money in Scott's soccer so he has to keep playing and moving to the next level."

"I put together this spreadsheet of addresses for holiday cards when the kids were little—it's mostly right so I'll keep using it."

When we believe we've invested time, and money, into a system, we are sometimes loathe to change it. It's part of our human nature to create elaborate workarounds for systems that are no longer tenable. We'd rather jump through hoops and create extra work for ourselves than admit we need to revisit the initial challenge and see if we can create something more useful. Like most people, I am in awe of the late Maya Angelou and the breadth and depth of her spirit. She said, "If you don't like something, change it. If you can't change it, change your attitude." When we let go of the story we create—both for our stuff and for our situation—it's much easier to see it for what it really is. That's what being adaptable means in our lives and our decision-making.

There are some simple ways to stay organized and current that do not require an elaborate system. Because knowing where you are—emotionally, financially, physically—is living your best life. Choose intentional actions. Create habits that keep you moving forward in your life. Open the mail and deal with it. Ignorance is not bliss; it's just ignorance. You are choosing to be unaware and disorganized and it's costing you time, money, and peace of mind. Start with something simple that also has huge impact: updating your records.

Do you have a new healthcare insurance provider? Did you make a switch on your auto or homeowner's insurance recently? For most of us, it's common to make these kinds of changes but updating our records and filing is not. Maybe we believe we've already created the perfect system and we are unwilling to revisit it. Creating an effective filing system for your working documents is critical—more on that to come—but you also need to maintain and update that system.

Organizing Tip

I urge clients to cull old files and create new ones that meet present needs. Sifting through files and paperwork to find what you really need is a waste of time. Make it easy to do it right

Being in an auto accident or needing to file a homeowners claim is stressful enough. Don't add more stress and frustration to your life by relying on your memory to remember that your current auto policy is housed in a file with the name of the previous insurance company. Because when you got the new policy, you just shoved it in the drawer with the old stuff and thought "I'll remember that when I need it." Will you? Why would you leave that to chance? Create a new, updated file. Take the two minutes now to create and update your file. Save yourself twenty minutes the next time looking for a misfiled item. Now that you have updated your files, what other items need attention?

I strongly recommend that when new paperwork or updated items are received, immediately replace the old, outdated items. Insurance is a great example of this. Replace membership cards, policies, physical forms and other important documents as soon as you receive them. If you process your important paperwork immediately, there's no searching for missing/current items. Do you keep a binder of your child's current school information? Is your child heading to high school and you still have the fourth grade information in the book? Purge, purge, purge. Is your child a practiced driver and you still have the driver's ed material on your counter? Throw it out. Replace old, outdated information with new, current content. This is not memorabilia. It is clutter. Be merciless when it comes to holding onto old documents and be sure to shred anything with a social security number, date of birth, or other critical information.

Review and update your files and information and only keep what is new and current. When my sons were in school, I kept a three-ring binder for each in the kitchen. The binder was color coded and had the current school grade. In went sports team info, class lists, and the current school year's course information. The class schedule, copies of birth certificates,

Organizing Tip

These binders are a great spot to store "in process" paperwork for your student. Order forms for school photos or the book fair live here. Anything I ordered and was waiting on for delivery went in the binder. When the item was received or the task completed, the paperwork was recycled. No more sifting through piles of paperwork and trying to remember contact info or upcoming dates; it's sitting in the binder waiting for you.

and medical forms lived in there so there was never any question of where to find the important information.

Any time the boys went for a physical, I made extra copies. One immediately went to the school to be put on record for school and high school athletics and the remainder lived in his binder. Copies of birth certificates were kept in the binder as well for team sports when this needed to be included with registration. No more searching around for the necessary documents—copies were always ready to go. Any medication information and copies of prescriptions lived there. Each family member knew where to go for his baseball schedule or team emails.

Organizing Tip

Yes, I know that most everything is online today, but I still recommend the binders for busy households. I have seen clients spend lots of time looking up schedules and information and trying to find the right content. If it exists in the binder, you save a boatload of time and effort.

Once the boys were in high school and college, there wasn't a need to keep as much content so it became less about schoolwork and more about real work: applications submitted, paperwork outstanding, etc. But I still use and recommend a Kitchen Folio or binder with current content for every household. This is also a great spot for new and updated phone numbers for easy access for the entire family. Regardless of the chatter about the benefits of a "paperless" society, sometimes having important information printed and readily available make my life easier.

16

Taking off the Badge of Busy

"Life is what happens when you are busy making other plans."

—**John Lennon**

Have you ever run into a friend or acquaintance and when you ask "How are you? How are things going?" and the response is "Busy!" Or "Busy. But it's a good busy!" Guilty. For many years, I was so focused on the "doing of the doing" that I sometimes failed to pay attention to the why and be intentional. So, what does this mean for all of us? In our manic society that always seems time deprived, busy has become the new sign of success. If I'm busy, I must be productive! If I'm busy, I look and feel more important! If I say I'm not busy, will I appear lazy and unmotivated? But is any of that really accurate?

With many of my clients, and myself included, we get lazy

with our language and "busy" has become a catch-all phrase like "fine" or "good." With our multiple responsibilities and often hectic lives, this phrase also has become a shield and a barrier to deeper connection and an intentional life. As animals, we are hardwired for connection. Research has shown that we're most successful when we are engaged and involved with others—packs, tribes, clans, communities, etc. But the "busy" label keeps others at a distance and keeps us from that connection.

In *The Four Agreements* the author Don Miguel Ruiz addresses how we use language in our lives. Ruiz believes that language and how we speak is so important that he designates it as the first of the agreements. He urges the reader to be impeccable with your word, speak with integrity and say only what you mean. Is "busy" the impeccable way to describe your day? I sometimes have to stop myself and think of a better way to describe my time. Stacked. Productive. Energized. Excited. These are words that allow engagement and invite interest, for myself and others.

Instead of the lazy language of "busy," what other way can you describe your time? Tell yourself that you are engaged, excited, and motivated and you will be pleasantly surprised to find that this is the case. Tell yourself you are *so* busy and frantic, and it will be so. Do you have to "fake it until you make it"? Sometimes it's more about how we describe a situation than the situation itself. Ask yourself: What the heck am I so busy doing? There is no doubt that we are often over-scheduled and our lives seem more demanding than those of previous generations. So it seems that we are busier than ever. But that's not really accurate. Up until World War II and the

Organizing Tip

Are you feeling very busy in your life? Can you say *exactly* what you are so busy with? Go back and revisit the time prioritization section in Chapter 12. Yes, we all have blocks or chunks of time that are more demanding than others, like the "morning rush" or the dreaded "dinner, homework, and bedtime" block. Are there shifts you can make to move some tasks around to even out the workload?

great migration into the cities, most of the population of the US lived in rural communities. In these communities, farm life was much more demanding, both physically and from a time perspective. Now, we have more leisure time than ever before. In so many ways, our lives are so much easier than our predecessors. Yet we act as if we are busy tilling the land, protecting the homestead, and eking out a subsistence life—all not true. Ask instead: What am I so busy doing?

I have worked with many wonderful clients over the years. And a great majority of them defined themselves as busy or very busy. Some clients have even described their lives as frenetic and chaotic, which can create a lot of stress and unhappiness. Certain situations will cause a truly busy time in our lives. Life events like weddings, graduations, illness, new parenting, and moves will quicken the pace of our ordinary days. Is that the case with you? Or, are you in a constant state of "busy," leading to burnout and unhappiness?

The answer to this question is at the heart of intentional living. Are you busy with classes, education, volunteering, and vocational work? Great—that level of being busy should feel productive and satisfying. When you're living intentionally, you take off the badge of busy and you are responsible for and to your decisions.

Does it feel uncomfortable and difficult to look at your busyness? Many clients who struggle with disorganization have a difficult time understanding or examining why they are "busy being busy." Decide to "take off the badge of busy" and rewrite the story of your life. The reality is that we sometimes use tasks and situations to keep from examining our lives and decisions more closely. Could I be running to stay ahead of that level of introspection? What if I slow down and stop working myself into the ground while not feeling like I'm accomplishing anything at all? Do I then have to address my underlying unhappiness or discontent with my relationships, my work, and my life? If I stop the frantic pace of running, running, running, will I have to face my fears and questions about where I am in my life and where I'm going?

Are you busy with social media, Netflix, and shopping that leaves you dissatisfied and unhappy? What can you do less of or differently? The busy pattern you see and experience is sometimes the result of avoidance and denial, not having too much to do. In his 7 *Habits of Highly Effective People*, Steven Covey talks a lot about what our priorities say about us. "The way you spend your time is a result of the way you see your time and the way you really see your priorities."[6] Everyone needs to relax and rejuvenate; a lazy Sunday sleeping late and watching Netflix has its place after a hectic few weeks. Take time for yourself. Do something that makes you feel rejuvenated. Use this as an opportunity to get started again with new energy and more motivation. In an intentional life, this is the exception, not the rule.

Busy with the new season of your go-to reality TV show? Busy with spending a Saturday shopping for tchotchkes to fill your already cluttered home? Busy subscribing to more magazines you'll never read? Are those things bringing you joy? Do those activities and things lead to a fulfilled life? Ask yourself: Am I creating "busy" when it doesn't need to exist? This pattern of creating more busyness is really about us, not others' demands on us. Are you spending five hours baking and decorating the "perfect" birthday cake when a store-bought one will do? Is decorating your home for the holidays demanding so much of your time that you are unable to enjoy the "reason for the season"? Are you so busy creating an Instagram- and Pinterest-worthy life that you make yourself frantic in the process? That's not being busy. That's *choosing* busy. If these activities truly brought you joy, you'd feel that way, not just busy. If you are doing these things for others' praise and accolades or the dreaded #humblebrag, stop.

Organizing Tip

If busy is your default state, it's time to slow down and reassess how you're spending your time. An organizing or life coach can provide some perspective on how to better prioritize your time and tweak your schedule.

You're doing this to yourself and throwing away your time. If your default status is "busy," but you are unfulfilled, stressed, and unhappy, it's time for an internal audit. Revisit your priorities and start living intentionally.

CHAPTER

17

Distractions and the Social Media Time Suck

"It takes discipline not to let social media steal your time."

—Alexis Ohanian

What is your biggest distraction? Is it the phone, email, social media, or constant interruptions from others? How many times have you been in the middle of a conversation and your phone rings, or beeps, or vibrates, taking you out of the moment and you lose your train of thought? Or you're working on a task or project, either at home or in the office, and a tweet or text comes in.

You stop what you're doing to "check it" and when you look up again, you've just spent (or wasted) twenty minutes. In organizing, I like to use an analogy from a favorite children's book, *If You Give a Mouse a Cookie*. In the story, everything the mouse touches and encounters leads him in another direction. The mouse is easily distracted, always onto something else, resulting in lost time and lots of disorganization. He is beset by distraction after distraction and he and the boy lose a whole day with these interruptions. So ... are you like the mouse?

In some ways, each of us is like the mouse. We all have distractions in our everyday lives that keep us from finishing a task or project in a timely manner. I am at my desk working to finish a project that my boss needs by this afternoon. The phone rings and I am expecting a call from a client so I answer the phone. Except it's not the client; it's a friend wanting to catch up. I know I need to get back on task but I've been meaning to call this friend anyway so I stay on the phone. And then the call does come in from the client so I take that call. After the client call, I remember I need to firm up with my partner about plans for the evening so we start a fifteen-minute, back-and-forth text session. A colleague stops by on her way to lunch, so I go and join her because hey, everybody needs to eat. On the way back to my desk from lunch, I remember I need a new computer cable so I head to IT and end up chatting with a co-worker there. When I finally return to my desk, I spend a "few minutes" catching up on social media and checking on my fantasy team. Before I know it, it's 5:00 p.m. and the project is not completed. Hello, mouse.

Managing and minimizing distractions are key elements of organization and time prioritization. Whether you are trying to focus on a project at work or complete a task at home, constant distractions slow us down significantly. It's the constant stopping and restarting of our projects that slows progress and expands the timeline. The longer it takes to get the job completed, the more stress I am adding. This holds true for most any task; making lunches or completing an expense report or cleaning out my closet. Clear, uninterrupted focus on the task at hand means it will be completed in much less time.

Let's be clear. I live in the real world just like you. I am often required to stop what I'm doing and address someone else's priority all the time. That's real life. When you have little ones at home or work in a particularly demanding environment, getting tasks completed is one of our greatest challenges. When we're talking about health and safety, there is no question about which priority to address in that moment. But are we always talking about health and safety?

We all deal with distractions in our day and sometimes these distractions can lead to feeling stressed and disorganized. I can't stay focused on organizing my pantry because of so many interruptions and disorganization sets in. My office becomes cluttered and unworkable because every time I try to purge and edit my files, I'm interrupted and my attention is diverted. I believe we all have some distractions that pull us off task. The key is to be clear and intentional on the goal of the task. If that goal does not have strong and commanding value for you, you will always find something else that will distract you and pull you away like my friend the mouse.

Organizing Tip

Set the timer on your phone for a reasonable length of time—forty-five to sixty minutes. Research from a study at the University of Illinois at Urbana-Champaign determined that after about fifty minutes, our ability to concentrate and be creative and productive drops significantly.[7] So "powering through" a three-hour writing session might be possible, but you may not end up with the best product. After the timer goes off, take a 5 minute break. Hit the bathroom, grab a healthy snack, and hydrate; and then get started again.

So, how do I minimize distractions to stay motivated and on task? Try a "do not disturb" mentality. One by one, shut down your distractions. Turn the ringer off on your phone or set to "do not disturb"—don't worry, the timer alarm will still go off. Minimize the taskbar that shows that a new email has come in. Place your phone upside down so you won't see texts or notifications coming in. Are you concerned you might miss an "urgent" message? Set your phone to alarm after twenty or thirty minutes for a quick peek to be sure there is nothing that warrants your immediate attention. Are you in open office space and can't close your door for a short period of time to work on a critical task? Move into a conference room or put on ear buds to block out distractions.

At home with your family, giving yourself a "time out" or "do not disturb" period will be more difficult. If you are co-parenting, let your partner know you will be focusing on cleaning out the closet for the next hour. Can she handle any kid requests during that time so you can be done sooner? If there isn't another adult in the home, trade off care time with a friend or neighbor to make the most of your focus time. The key to making this scenario work is to communicate that you need time to focus on a project. If you can be behind closed doors, even better. Just don't ghost. Don't disappear and not inform your partner or co-workers why you are not available. The goal is to complete the task in the shortest amount of time possible; that's the incentive for uninterrupted and non-distracted time. The more focus you can have, the less time you will need. Isn't that motivation enough for everyone involved?

I am more productive and less stressed when I manage my time and distractions. Figure out what solutions work best for you to filter out your distractions and keep going. There aren't too many people who enjoy organizing the playroom or finishing data analysis for a meeting; these tasks still need to be completed anyway. The timeworn belief that we just need willpower to push through uncomfortable and boring tasks is no longer as credible. The reality is that while we all have some level of willpower, it is not limitless. If you've used a lot of willpower to get in an early morning workout, make several challenging client calls, and have a difficult conversation with a colleague, how much willpower do you think is left to power through completing your pile of paperwork before distraction sets in? In her blog post, "Here's My Habits Manifesto. What's Yours?", Gretchen Rubin remarked that it's easier to change our surroundings than ourselves. In addition to employing willpower, you can also control your environment to minimize distractions and set yourself up to be more successful.

Personally, one of my biggest time prioritization challenges is social media. For most of us, social media, in all of its many manifestations, is a part of our daily lives. For anyone in marketing, sales, or communications, it is a necessary evil. For the rest of us, social media can be a fun distraction, a communication tool, and definitely a "time suck" that drains our time and productivity. Have you ever said, "I'll just check Facebook *for five minutes*," and you look up from the screen and an hour has gone by without your even noticing? Social media, for all its useful applications, is absolutely a rabbit hole we can all fall into. When we are engaged with social media, we are not engaged with what's going on around us. This takes us out of the present and we lose time. In the workplace, the stakes and costs are even higher. Studies from the digital marketplace have shown a 13 percent loss in productivity in the workplace due to social media use;[8] this costs the economy billions each year. So, how do I keep social media from being a time and productivity suck?

The Greek poet Hesiod urged, "Moderation is best in all things." Limit social media if you want to remain productive and on schedule—at home and at work. Too much of anything is not healthy, so put yourself on a social media "diet." Resist the temptation to click on interesting links or check out what others are doing and saying online. Like resisting cupcakes is good for

Organizing Tip

Set a timer on your phone and when the timer goes off, get off social media.
If you are truly on social media for work, write some bullet points on what you are doing and stick to your outline.

your waistline, resisting our friends' feeds is good for your productivity.

Turn social media notifications off on your phone to keep from logging on constantly. Like Pavlov's dog, we hear that little "ding" and think the message is something we must check out immediately. Instead, set a time each day to go through your social media feeds and engage online. A couple of hours will not make a difference in liking a friend's photo. Some folks really struggle with wasting time on social media and games, especially on their phones. If you find it a distraction you cannot manage, remove the social media apps from your phone altogether. By doing this, you will "find" significant blocks of time each day. If this feels very overwhelming, try removing apps one by one and go slowly. Like nicotine withdrawal, social media withdrawal may feel difficult at first but the benefits are significant.

In addition to gaining more time during the day, limiting or disengaging from social media has other positive benefits as well. Studies have shown that a person who spends more than an hour a day on social media experiences much more negativity and lower self-esteem than less frequent users. The belief behind the study is that because the nature of Facebook and Instagram is to showcase the highlights and victories of life, we negatively compare ourselves and our lives to what we see online. The result is that we feel bad about ourselves, feeling our lives don't measure up. Also, with the divisive and negative political environment played out on social media, we get caught up in this negativity constantly. Mark Manson, author of *The Subtle Art of Not Giving a F*ck: A Counterintuitive Approach to Living a Good Life*, had strong feelings on the negativity of social media. "People get addicted to feeling offended all the time because it gives them a high; being self-righteous and morally superior feels good."

As humans, we are hardwired for connection and social media especially feels like a community, a community we can access at any time. While certainly there are many positives to social media, it is also our responsibility to manage it. Would you like it if twenty "friends" barged into your house while you are making dinner and helping the kids with homework? Would that help you finish the task more quickly and efficiently? When I am under a deadline to get important data to a colleague for a presentation, is it okay for my cousin's best friend's son to distract me by showing me a funny cat video? I don't think so. And yet we allow these things to happen when we don't manage and control social media and other distractions. You have control over your time and how you use it. Use it wisely.

18

Write It Down and Get It Done

"Dooley noted...."

—Lisa Dooley

*L*ong before starting my organizing practice, I lived and breathed my to-do list. In the middle of the controlled chaos that was sometimes my life, this little bit of sanity kept me grounded and feeling on track. I cannot overstate the value of a to-do list. When I start with a new client who is struggling with disorganization, one of my first questions is "Where's your to-do list?"

Surprisingly, this simple organizing practice is often overlooked. What's the value of a list? A to-do list allows us to get all that stuff that's swirling around in our heads out of there. This saves incredible amounts of time in creating the beginning of order and organization. Most of us are presented each day with multiple responsibilities—home, work, community, kids—and keeping track of all the things we have to do is challenging. Putting it down on "paper"—either writing it or using an electronic process—makes those tasks more concrete so that we can make time to get it done.

How do I best use a to-do list? Here again, it's best to decide between a paper or an electronic list. Some clients choose an electronic to-do list on a phone or tablet because it's portable and always available wherever they are. However, for me, it takes me more time to open the app or program, type the task, and then save and close the app/program than it does to jot down a task on a written list. Also, you have to repeat the process to delete a task from your electronic list. Creating an electronic shopping list is a must for some folks. That way it is always available on your device when you are out shopping and you don't have to rely on a list kept at home.

Figure out what works for you—try a combination; there is no right or wrong. You don't have to apologize or justify your system. Just create some sort of system. For me, a written list works best—all I need is a notepad and a pen. In my office, I use a yellow legal pad for a daily to-do list for work tasks. This allows me flexibility to move tasks to different days as needed. I also keep a to-do pad in the kitchen. Every task is not a "right now" task. If I am in the middle of completing a work project or proposal, but remember I need to order checks, I put that task on the list. It needs to get done but it doesn't need to be completed right now. Again, this is time prioritization at its best.

We all have a myriad of responsibilities and to dos, both for long- and short-term. Are you feeling overwhelmed by all the tasks you have to complete and you don't know where

Organizing Tip

Are you familiar with the "two-minute rule"? With clients who struggle with time prioritization and task completion, this is a powerful process that I coach. While most tasks can be added to a to-do list and handled at a later time, some tasks are important enough to do right away. If the task will truly take two minutes to complete, do it now. That might be sending a confirmation text or email or changing a light bulb. Run your task through this filter: "Can I do it in two minutes and will it positively impact me right now?" *I need to confirm a meeting for the morning; great, send the text so you can plan your schedule for tomorrow.*

to begin? Start your organizing process by doing a "brain dump." Use a yellow legal pad and write down a different task to be completed on each page. The process of writing it down helps and once you start, you'll be amazed at all the things you remember need doing. Then sit down and run through the stack, creating "now" and "not now" piles. Complete the "now" items immediately; schedule time for this!

Any tasks/sheets not finished add to your to-do list. The effectiveness of this process comes from the actual doing of the tasks; there is no short cut to this. I know, I know … this is not the greenest organizational tip so use it sparingly. There is nothing more satisfying after completing a task on the sheet than crumpling up that piece of paper and recycling it. This is a very close second to crossing out something on your to-do list!

As an organizing process, utilizing a to-do list is a simple yet extremely powerful tool. Have you ever tried to get through a full day of commitments and remember all the tasks and projects you need to complete? For most of us, the answer is a resounding "yes." So, how successful were you in getting everything done in a timely and efficient manner? Sadly, most of us will answer "no" to that question.

It's extremely challenging to remember all the tasks and responsibilities we need to manage. To be more efficient, you need to write it down. The task of writing in itself creates muscle memory and reinforces the reminder. When you write down your tasks and projects, you jog your memory to complete the task. Equally important, you create a visual reminder of tasks to be incorporated into your schedule. A written, visible to-do list is really effective for some of us as it is always "in your face."

When we are less stressed and not bogged down with our stuff, we can find more space, more time, and more joy in our lives. That's the *why* that drives the process. How you get there is less important and can take many different forms. For some clients, a PDA or smartphone is a must for everything from grocery lists to work tasks. Written lists, sometimes scratched on the back of junk mail, do the trick for others. For visual learners especially, a written note has significant impact. I have a "special" notepad in my kitchen and legal pads in my office to write down reminders. Whatever works for you works for you. Where are your strategic areas for notes?

You save time, money, and effort when you have a to-do list. Many clients I've worked with have consistently paid late and penalty fees because they don't pay bills on time or are late with activity sign-ups. Why? Because we have so much going on that we forget to complete these small but critical tasks. We all want to feel accomplished and that we are getting things done. "Focus on actions, not on outcomes."[9] Using a to-do list is a simple process to make that happen. Write down your tasks so you can see the progress you are making and what needs to be done next. In creating a to-do list and a system, choose the process that works best for you. No one can remember all the tasks we need to complete—write it down to get it done.

Another great visual reminder is the sticky note, again in a strategic place. I have the same routine every day when I wake up; I am truly a creature of habit. When I need to remind myself of something that is a deviation from that morning routine, I need to see it immediately upon waking. To be sure I don't miss the reminder, I put it right on my bedroom mirror. Another critical spot for me is the kitchen table—I see it when I go to the kitchen for water and coffee first thing. I have also put sticky notes on the door so my sons don't forget something if I am gone in the morning before them. Hey, whatever it takes! Because we are creatures of habit, putting a sticky note where we can't fail to see it is a visual reminder that represents a change in routine or reinforces a new habit.

Some clients really love using sticky notes as reminders— these are often visual learners and "creatives" (you know who you are). While this concept is positive, be cautious about too many sticky notes; especially stuck all over your desk or computer space, which can lose their effectiveness and become visual clutter. There really is such a thing as "too much of a good thing." They become overwhelming and we literally stop seeing them.

When you write down a reminder or task, you create a visual system that is a trigger for action. Use notes, lists, and sticky notes to create an organizing system that makes your time more efficient.

I make my time more efficient and myself more effective when I value my time. In Chapter 12, I talk about time prioritization versus the old standard of time management. Living intentionally and with more space, more time, and more joy in my life is not about finding more time to get things done. It's about doing those things that lead me into my best and fullest life. The ancient philosopher Lao Tzo said, "Nature does not hurry, yet everything is completed." Am I better than nature? Rarely.

In addition to prioritizing your time, focus on the difference between important and urgent tasks. Do you use the terms *important* and *urgent* interchangeably? Many people do, but there are subtle and important differences. So, what's the difference between important and urgent tasks in time prioritization? If a task is urgent, complete it immediately. Urgent tasks that are safety and health related are most important so don't delay on doing these right away. That might be the task of replacing the batteries in the smoke detector or scheduling a health care visit. If a task has a near deadline or involves health and safety, do it now.

Have I mentioned that I'm a real person just like you? I have children that needed to be fed, driven to practice, and responded to *immediately*. My husband starts many conversations with "Are you are at your desk?" which loosely translates to, "I need you to do something for me...." I have had sick and passing family members. Phones ring. Emails come in. Texts abound. And oh yeah, that working with clients thing happens ... I live in the real world just like you. I know what it's like to juggle multiple responsibilities at the same time with competing urgencies—my phrase for that is "controlled chaos." Even in the midst of all this, I know that I control the pace and rhythm of my life.

I choose what task to focus on. I am *proactive*, not *reactive*. Instead of bouncing from one crisis to another and always feeling stressed and overwhelmed, slow down. Not every situation or task—especially those deemed "urgent and important" by others—requires that you act on it immediately. I don't know who first uttered this quote but it resonates with this theme. "Lack of planning on your part does not constitute an emergency on my part." Be intentional.

But aren't important tasks urgent too? Sometimes yes; and sometimes no. Looking at your to-do list, I know you have lots of tasks that you need to complete both personally and professionally. You remember that your friend's anniversary is next week and you want to send a card. Great, put it on the to-do list but don't interrupt the project you're working on to complete that task. This is important but not urgent. You remember that your niece's birthday is today—so it's both important and urgent. Using the "Two-Minute Rule," you send a quick text message wishing her a happy birthday and write on your to-do list to send a gift. You're working on the report for your boss that has to be completed by end of day and you remember you need to follow up on upcoming summer vacation plans. You add "call the hotel and check flights" to the to-do list, but keep working on your project. A colleague sends an email to you and several others to change a meeting time for this afternoon; send a quick response to the sender only and get back to work.

Organizing Tip

Go back and re-read Chapter 17 on minimizing distractions. The buzz of activity and constant interruptions we are faced with are significant. When I start rushing around and feel frazzled, I breathe deep and refocus. Remember Lewis Carroll's advice from the White Rabbit. "The hurrier I go, the behinder I get.

You have lots of important tasks to complete so build time into your schedule so they don't become urgent crises. I work on certain tasks early in the morning when I have uninterrupted time before the "work day" starts and the phone starts ringing. I use this uninterrupted time to complete important tasks—writing, blogging, and other focus-intensive projects—when the day is quiet. Every task is not urgent; learn to discern the difference between important and urgent.

Good time prioritization keeps most important tasks from becoming urgent tasks. Yes, things will come up and you will need to redirect your focus, but this should be the exception, not the rule. Time is a limited commodity. Use it wisely in order to accomplish more and have more time for the people and things you love.

19

Working and Historical Files and Forever Documents

"That which we persist in doing becomes easier—not that the nature of the task has changed, but our ability to do it has increased."

—Ralph Waldo Emerson

Organizing is finding my stuff when I need it; that's it. The staged photo spreads you see in magazines of organized spaces are just that: staged. Create and maintain organizing systems that work in your home and office and then go do something fulfilling that leads you to your best life.

There's lots of stuff we need to organize in our lives and this includes a lot of paperwork. Over the years I have worked with many clients, both residential and business owners, on creating and maintaining filing systems. This is an area of organization that we all need but one which we defer a lot. Because it's time-consuming. Because we don't know where to start. Because it's *boring*.

Is your filing a mess? Have you neglected to update and maintain your once organized system? Stop deferring and putting off this task; it has significant value financially, emotionally, and psychologically. Ready to get started? This is one area of organizing in which I highly recommend purchasing supply products. With other organizing categories, choosing the "container" is more flexible, but with filing, there really is only one way to go. Invest in sturdy, quality, hanging files and new file folders to create an effective system. Nothing makes finding your important documents more of a challenge than broken, ripped, and overstuffed folders.

Spend time planning your system and ask the question: "What documents do I really need handy?" Well, that depends. Have you ever tried to find your health care forms or insurance policy in a crisis? Can you put your hands on your bank statements or mortgage documents in an instant? If you can, congratulations—you have an effective set of *working* documents. But for many, this is an unlikely scenario. Working documents are those items you need to be able to "touch" on a consistent basis—think weekly or monthly. Find a list of common working documents on my website—this is a good place to start for planning your filing system. These common items include current insurance policies for auto, home, health care, etc. Keep only current policies so that you're not confused about what is in effect. Organize bank, mortgage, and investment statements for easy referral. Health care and insurance documents need to be easy to locate. When you receive the new, updated documents, get rid of the old ones. Do not hold onto expired policies—there is no value other than clogging up your filing system.

So, how should you organize your files? To create a practical filing system, think intuitively. Start by going through your existing files and deciding which files you need to keep. This purging and weeding out is often an initial stumbling block for many clients because it's tedious and time-consuming. Pull out all your files and go through them one by one. Yes. All the files.

Do you have a file for your current bank and investment accounts? Great. Go through the file and remove anything you no longer need. What falls into this category is pretty broad but includes things like old statements, canceled checks, and any marketing materials. Shred anything with account information or a social security number. This is an instance where it is better to err on the side of caution. Due to

Organizing Tip

Ideally, keep your working documents in a traditional filing cabinet for easiest access. If you lack space for even a small, two drawer filing cabinet, use clear, plastic filing boxes. You can find these at any home goods or office supply store. Don't skimp on quality so you can create effective working files.

Organizing Tip

Do not stop and shred each document as you go! This is incredibly time-consuming and will slow down your project immeasurably. Just put your pile of to-be-shredded aside. If you don't own a shredder, you can take these to your local office supply store and they shred by the pound for a very reasonable rate.

the many issues around identity theft and account hacking, shredding is your best option. Use recyclable brown paper bags and fill them with your shredding.

Once you've purged your files of unwanted and unneeded extra content, you'll be down to the working documents you need to access on a consistent basis. Do your current files contain all of your updated and necessary files? For instance, you might have purchased a home since you last updated your files and now you need to keep track of property taxes, water bills, mortgage statements, etc. Create new files for these important documents.

Organizing Tip

Think about how you will look for these files when you need them. Does it make sense to call the file "mortgage statements" or "ABC Bank Mortgage"? Will you look for information on your new car under "Auto" or "Nissan Sentra"? This is your filing system; set it up so it works for you.

Let's talk for a minute about what files to keep here and what can go out of your working documents. Again, this is a highly personal decision that you need to make about your files. The "rule of thumb" is to hold onto personal tax returns for seven years and business returns and paperwork for ten years. You can review the IRS regulations on document retention at www.irs.gov. These regulations cover both individuals and businesses and you should take the time to review them if you have any questions about how long or what to keep.

While you do need to keep some documents for a longer period of time, they do not necessarily need to be kept in your working files. Your working files are files you need to access on a weekly or monthly basis. Anything that is not current I refer to as *historical* documents. Historical documents include tax returns from prior years, refinanced mortgage documents, or documents on the sale of a previous home. These can be stored in another location so that they are not clogging up your working files and making your system unmanageable. Weed out these historical documents and house them in a different spot. Now you have your true working documents. Let's get started on getting them into an organized system.

True confession: I love label makers and I own three. When I am creating a new filing system or doing updates to an existing system, I print out the labels for the hanging files and the file folders. The look is clean, uncluttered, and easy to read. There is nothing more frustrating than trying to find the right information when the files have crossed out, scribbled, and re-used lettering. This is not a spot to reduce, reuse, and recycle.

Recycle the old filing supplies but invest in new products—it is definitely worth the cost. Do you like fancy, decorative files and feel that having them will motivate you to maintain your filing system? Then get the pretty, fancy products. This is *your* system and your life; you don't have to justify or explain your decisions to anyone. Gandhi said, "The future depends on what you do today." Figure out what works for you today. Just get it done.

Either with a label maker or with clear printing, create hanging folders and file folders with clear, accurate tabs so finding your information is quick and easy. In an office setting, use a traditional filing cabinet with multiple drawers whenever possible. This is the optimal solution so that it can be accessed by others in the office. Again, if your small business (or your home filing) does not have the space, use plastic filing bins. I do not recommend cardboard bankers boxes. While they may start out organized and easy to use, these boxes are not conducive to easily maintaining your filing system. These do not stand up over time and make filing difficult. Use these cardboard boxes when storing historical files for longer term storage. Since you won't need to frequently (or ever) refer back to these files, you don't need to be concerned about how well the boxes are being managed.

In addition to old and historical files, what else doesn't belong in your working files? Purchased product information, including installation and warranty content, should be removed from your filing system.

I have seen many filing systems with ripped, broken, and overflowing files for purchased items the client no longer owns. Again, I recommend either a heavy-duty, expanding A-Z file folder or another bin for all this content. I like the expanding file because I can alphabetize the contents and find the warranty and repair info on my dishwasher in seconds. Again, putting all that content in a bin is fine as well. Write on the manual the purchase date and amount and staple the receipt to it. Since you will need to access this file very infrequently, store it where you store your electronics bin—out of the way but still available when needed.

Filing Systems for a True Renaissance Man

One of my first clients was an entrepreneur who owned a number of successful businesses as well as multiple rental properties. W. was a true renaissance man, deeply involved in his community and with his family and a number of local endeavors. What W. was not was organized. Years of growing his businesses had left him with a significant need to organize his files and paperwork. His home office had become a bit of a dumping ground for paperwork, which had proliferated, and the manila folders were piled up all over the space. "Hidden" in the resulting heaps were documents and files that were much needed.

Whew! Did I mention that W. was one of my first clients? I'd be lying if I didn't say the scene when he first opened that door was pretty overwhelming ... for me. The first step in dismantling the years of neglected files? Literally digging through the piles.

(continued)

Facing such a big filing project, we started by segmenting out the different groupings, by businesses, properties, community projects, etc. We dug into each file folder and replaced any that weren't in good shape. Because this filing project covered such diverse segments, we chose to use different colored manila folders to signify the appropriate group. (For most filing projects, this won't be necessary, but if you are working with multiple properties and businesses like this, colored folders are a super easy way to differentiate.) We also were lucky to have multiple filing drawers to put the different projects, so we utilized this additional way to break down the files.

For each file—and there were about 150—using the label maker for the file names wasn't feasible as it was too slow. Instead I wrote in pencil on each file folder and created a list to be typed later. In Word, there are options to type and print file labels—quicker and less expensive than using a label maker. (Again, you will likely not have so many labels to write so it's a nonstarter, but it is a good option for a high volume or if you don't have a label maker—you do you.)

The goal of this project was to create order and organization. By segmenting the files by property and business, we were able to locate the corresponding paperwork for each and then add any appropriate expenses to the files. This project was significant and took over twenty hours to complete—do not underestimate the amount of time it will take to organize your office!

(continued)

New clients routinely believe this filing project will take "a couple hours, tops." Maybe. But likely not. You need to invest the time to make this happen. The result of this work? A clear, organized filing system that was workable and adaptable to growth which is always a great goal. The client was thrilled with the outcome and his response reflected the amazing value such a project brings. "I have rarely filed my taxes on time because of all of these moving parts but now I can." Nailed it.

For your working files, invest in good quality folders and storage. Being able to find your working documents quickly and easily is critical to making your life less stressful. Once a year, update your filing system to be sure that all your files are up to date and current. The New Year is a great time to review your system and remove last year's receipts, statements, and paperwork and ensure your system is ready for the next calendar year. And it's winter. Grab a cup of coffee or tea and spend the thirty minutes updating and purging your files—you'll thank yourself in March when it's tax season.

The key to maximizing the effectiveness of your working files comes from maintaining it. Being consistent in my filing makes it easier for me down the road. In her blog, "Here's My Habits Manifesto. What's Yours?", Gretchen Rubin reiterates the value of daily consistency. "What we do every day matters more than what we do once in a while." By making choices that align with your values, you stay consistent. By keeping your working documents in a well-organized filing system that you use on a regular basis, you can find your stuff when you need it. Voilá! Organized.

Take a minute to review the list of working and historical documents you created for your filing system—you'll find my copy in the Resources section and on my website. Again, these are files you need to access on a consistent basis. But what about the other important, vital documents you have? Where should you keep them and for how long?

Do you know you have documents you should always hold on to? Everyone does. I call these *forever* documents. Examples are birth certificates, social security cards, military discharge and citizenship papers. Find a list of common working documents in the Resources section of this book and on my website—this is a good place to start for planning your filing system. Are you married? If so, your original marriage certificate is a forever document (as are divorce decrees). Keep this securely along with your will and estate documents. Are you a parent or guardian? Guardianship documents and adoption papers are forever documents. Did you purchase a home and take out a Homestead Act? This is an important forever document so store this paperwork securely along with deeds to your property and mortgage discharge notices. Do you have a passport? Store your passport with your forever documents. Do not "tuck" your passport in a drawer or desk somewhere! Your passport is a critical legal document and is difficult and expensive to replace when lost or misplaced. Essentially, forever documents are records that provide proof of citizenship, critical personal information, and legal standing. Handle and treat them with care and respect.

Organizing Tip

I recommend that you store forever documents in a portable, firesafe box. You need to access forever documents rarely, generally only a few times a year. Invest in a quality, firesafe box which price at around $75 and are available at office supply stores and Amazon. Store your box in an accessible but not visible spot.

Note: Changes are being enacted in every state regarding state IDs, which now must meet federal standards for air travel even within the United States. Be prepared to produce your social security card, birth certificate, and passport for renewals in some states.

Forever documents should be stored separately from your working documents for a number of reasons. Unlike working documents which you access on a weekly or monthly basis, you "touch" forever documents very infrequently. My friend's son was starting his first real job and his employer required an original social security card for the new hire paperwork. My friend, a very organized person, went right to her "Social Security Card" file in the filing cabinet with all her documents but the file was not there. She spent hours searching for it in other places, only to have to re-order an original card from the Social Security Administration because the employer was demanding an original. It was weeks later that she found the file folder—it had fallen into her "Southwest Airlines" file, and that was why she could not find it. How much time do you waste looking for things you can't find? How much stress do you cause yourself with your frustration? Put your critical and vital—i.e. forever—documents, in a separate, secure spot so you know where to find them when you need them.

Working and forever documents, and how to manage and store them, is a topic I cover quite often in seminars and presentations. I talk about this subject, while hardly sexy or exciting, because it is *so* important. We've all had instances when we just couldn't "put our hands" on a file or paperwork we really needed. In talking about forever documents, I've been asked about bank safe deposit boxes a number of times. While some clients prefer the safety and security of a bank safe deposit box, my opinion is that this is not always ideal. The downside of using a bank safe deposit box is limited access to the box due to bank hours, weekends, or holidays. Some clients keep a copy of vital documents in the home or office and the originals at the bank; again, decide on whatever works for you.

In an emergency, you want to have access to your forever documents. During one of my "Fix-it Fridays" live Facebook series dealing with a specific organizing topic or challenge I got a great question from a friend, our former nanny. Lori's question was for her niece who lived in Florida in the midst of a very active hurricane season and how she might be prepared for likely evacuations. What kind of things should you have ready to "grab and go" in this scenario? If you are in a situation where evacuations seem likely due to weather or disasters, a firesafe box with your vital documents is a must. (I believe it is a must for everyone but that's a decision for you to make.) Include a copy of all your insurance policies so if you have to vacate your home in a short amount of time, you just grab the box and go.

Portability is another reason I recommend a firesafe box. It is light enough to remove with you (about fifteen to twenty pounds), but heavy enough that a burglar is unlikely to lug it out. Tuck it under a bed, in the linen closet covered in towels, in the attic or basement in an out of the way spot. Most burglars are in and out of your home in under fifteen minutes. They are looking for cash, jewelry, prescription drugs, electronics, and firearms. By keeping your vital documents together, secured and out of sight, they are the most protected. Some clients prefer a larger box or safe bolted to the floor, ensuring

Organizing Tip

There are organizing and productivity specialists who work specifically in the area of paperwork management.
If getting your working and forever documents organized is a roadblock for you, find a professional who can guide you through this process. Check out NAPO.net to find a professional who can help you get this very important project completed.

that in a robbery, the box isn't going anywhere. And it isn't. But it also isn't going with you when you have to evacuate in a hurry and go through the safe and put all the documents into another container. There are risks inherent in either decision—you need to decide your comfort level.

However you decide to store your forever documents, gather them together and store them securely today. Please don't tell me you don't have time to complete this task. Make time for what's really valuable and important. Stop giving time to what isn't. No one wants to be searching for a social security card or birth certificate in a rush. Keep your forever documents stored securely and you'll save yourself a lot of stress and aggravation. Create and maintain a working and historical document filing system that really works.

20

Clearing out the Clutter

"Time flies. It's up to you to be the navigator."

—**Robert Orben**

What is clutter? Best described, clutter is anything that stands between you and the vision you have for your life. It's deferred decisions. It's that layer of stuff, physical, emotional, and psychological, that holds you back from living your best life. It's so much more than just the physical. Those repeated negative decisions you make in your relationships? Clutter. Your frustration and anxiety at work? Clutter. The thoughts and feelings that constantly say you don't deserve to be happy? Clutter. The decisions that have landed you in financial difficulty? Clutter. All of this clutter is time-consuming and robs us of our ability to live our authentic lives because we are so busy repeating these patterns over and over. Like the unopened mail piling up, or the overflowing basket of unused toys, negative patterns continue. So how do you make it stop?

We get rid of the clutter in our lives when we truly align our choices with our priorities and values. You can talk about getting healthy and being fit all day long, but when you eat the pizza or the burger, you are not aligned with your vision of fitness. You say that you want to be financially savvy and secure, yet you purchase unnecessary items because you're feeling bored, dissatisfied, *whatever*. You're filling your life with clutter: physical, emotional, and psychological. Your life—your home, your office, even your car—is a reflection of your mind and your thoughts. If those spaces are cluttered, it is generally an indication of a mind that's cluttered.

Here's the reality: It's hard to make good decisions and promote healthy habits if your home or office space is chaotic and in disarray. A cluttered and disorganized space does not promote calm and positive decision-making. Instead, it tends toward hyperactivity and making decisions that are reactive and often not in our best interest. If you want to live your best life and find balance, take control of your environment. Make the time to gain control over your space now so that your home and office offers you peace and rejuvenation—not stress and anxiety. Make an investment in yourself and your life.

Note: I am using the word investment here—this is an intentional choice. What we pay attention and give our focus to multiplies. Do you want more time, more space, and more joy? Invest in the process of making that happen. If you can't make this happen on your own, spend the money and hire a professional who can help. An organizer or coach will help you go deeper and help you build the systems and processes for living a life with more balance. Define your goals so that you can create a plan for success—an organizing professional can help you do that.

Get rid of the clutter and you'll be amazed at how much lighter you feel. Eliminating physical clutter allows you to clean out emotional clutter as well. Decluttering and organizing isn't about boxes and bins and how things look. It's about how you feel and live your life. I love this quote that is often attributed to the Indian mystic Rumi: "You were born with greatness. You were born with wings. You are not

Out with the Old, in with the New

I worked with an amazing business owner who ran a very successful company, which grew and grew under her leadership—C. is an amazing person and a great leader. But her office was filled with old files from past projects including projects that had not gone well and even included protracted litigation. In essence, she was filling her space with negative energy that inhibited her ability to move forward. We cleaned out the old to make room for the new: new energy, new opportunities, new growth.

Like many of us, C. had not taken the time to focus on how her space was working for her, or in this case, not working for her. The first step was a big purge of what did not belong: files, reports, books, and paperwork. As president of the company, she had responsibility for

(continued)

reviewing the financials which were housed in three-ring binders and they were multiplying. Yes, she had responsibility for the data but did they have to stay in her space? Thankfully no. We were able to locate locked file cabinets in another part of the office so we opened up that critical space for her. Next came files and paperwork that could be rehoused, shredded, or refiled.

Once we dealt with the paper clutter, we focused on the physical space itself. Was the office set up conducive to the greatest productivity? Could we rearrange the furniture in the space to better utilize the layout? You know that jumble of cords and wires you walk over every time you move in your office? We dealt with that as well. By simply repositioning the desk, we moved that wiring mess out of the way so it wasn't a physical impediment any longer. (Try it. Figure out where your outlets and wires are connected and see if you can't create more streamlined space.)

The last part of the project was to remove the other clutter that had accumulated. Awards, certificates, and other professional memorabilia had been piled up onto the horizontal surfaces. Up on the wall they went, making great use of the open vertical space as well as creating positive energy in the space by acknowledging C.'s personal and professional success. All the books and magazines she was hoping to read went home where she might actually have time to go through them. Unneeded and unused decorative items were either purged or repositioned to create the calm, welcoming environment she was going for. And C. is still going strong, rocking her personal and professional life.

meant for crawling, so don't. You have wings. Learn to use them and fly." Clutter keeps us stuck at a low level. There's energy associated with everything in our lives; that energy is either negative or positive. If your office is cluttered with old files and paperwork, you're keeping that old energy in your space.

One of the greatest challenges we face in streamlining our lives and our clutter, both physical and psychic, is email. Regardless of what "social media experts" are saying, email is not dead. It is still a primary mode of communication, especially for Baby Boomers and their offspring. In this day and age, who doesn't have an overloaded inbox? When we have a personal email (or two or three) and a work email, it's easy to get overloaded.

Remember how we created a filing system for email in Chapter 13? Once you've been using your more organized email system for a few months, be sure to update it. Like keeping working documents in good shape, email files and

Organizing Tip

Your car is an extension of your physical space; don't allow clutter to take over that space either. Take ten minutes to clear out the junk and return things to where they belong either at the office, in the house, or in the trash. Resist the temptation to use your car as a dumping ground for stuff you haven't managed yet. If you put something in your car to return to the store or drop off for donation, do it. And do it today. Write it on your to do list and get it done and out of your car.

folders need to be updated consistently. Go through and delete unneeded file folders.

You deserve a life that is uncluttered. We all manage multiple, and sometimes competing, priorities. Yup, that's real life. But being engaged and involved in our lives does not mean that our life must be cluttered. You can choose to live a purposeful and focused life. This really speaks to the heart of important versus urgent tasks and how we choose to show up and engage in our lives. All the many forms of clutter that show up in our lives are something that we have to actively manage so that we are in control of our time and priorities.

I know lots of people for whom the inbox is everything. What arrives there drives their day and their focus. And yes, the inbox is a tool for communication and collaboration, and in some roles like sales it's the "bottom line." But it's just that, a tool. When we allow email, tweets, texts, Instastories, Facebook messages, or any other form of communication to rule our day, we've lost that control and it all becomes clutter. In his book, *The Charge: Activating the 10 Human Drives that Make You Feel Alive*, Brendon Burchard puts it this way: "The inbox is nothing but a convenient organizing system for other people's agendas."

Focus on what's important to you in your day, moving you forward to living your best life. Be mindful of going down a cluttered rabbit hole that's moving you away from what's important.

III

More Joy

Do you remember the last time you
felt real joy? The joy of being in the
moment and present for yourself and
others? Did that moment include a
thing or a bauble? Probably not. Joy is
not something you can buy or find; it
lives within us.
Let's go joy hunting....

21

Making It All Work

"Yesterday is gone. Tomorrow has not yet come. We have only today. Let us begin."

—Mother Teresa

"What comes easy won't last and what lasts won't come easy." Do you remember the adults in your life saying this to you when you were growing up? Did it mean little to you then but really resonates with you now? Fortunately or unfortunately, we live in a society that expects and adulates immediate gratification. We've bought into the mindset of immediacy and now. Our consumer mentality reinforces the notion that we can buy whatever it is that we are "missing." Our happiness and joy are just a credit card swipe away. With overnight shipping and delivery for almost anything, we've become accustomed to satisfying our every desire with a quick purchase and speedy delivery.

But is that true? Can buying more things really make us happy? Research says no. While there is some fleeting, temporary "high" around acquiring something new, the long-term effect is negligible and often negative. The negativity comes from the cost of purchasing something we really didn't need as well as the hidden cost of adding to your existing clutter. The reality is that things that are truly valuable in life take time and effort to achieve. So, what's valuable to you? My values in life are education, personal and professional growth, strong relationships, healthy living, and yes, organization.

We all face challenges in life, some great and some small. "Adversity happens to everyone and though pain is inevitable, despair is optional."[10] No one is immune from illness and death, challenges and struggle. In the end, it's not the situation itself that really challenges us but our reaction to it. The reality is that many of our "troubles" in life are self-created. Letting bills pile up and ignoring your financial situation because you don't feel competent. Avoiding the personal and physical upkeep you should be doing in your life and not focusing on your wellness because you are unmotivated. Choosing not to invest in personal growth and enriching relationships because you don't see the value in yourself. Becoming stagnant in your career and professional growth because it's easier. These are all common issues that we face; and *they are the result of the choices we make.* And the solution for each and every one of them—regardless of other issues and circumstances—is the same. You must take intentional, methodical steps to reclaim a healthy, organized, financially and emotionally fit, life.

If you choose not to be intentional with your decisions and actions, you will end up with your default life. And likely, your default life is not one that brings you joy and fulfill-ment. It's the life you end up with when you don't set goals for living your best life and then take action on those goals. Your mindset and actions must be aligned so you can drop the stories and excuses that have held you back up until this point. This is emotional clutter—the stories and the excuses that are holding you down and holding you back.

Yes, there will be times of challenge that seem uniquely diffi-cult. You will experience setbacks that will slow your prog-ress and derail you, at least in the short-term. But these situa-tions are not insurmountable; they serve to strengthen us and provide an opportunity to grow so that we can find our joy.

There is no magic wand, no quick fix, and no trip to the Container Store (however much fun that is!) that is going to get your life uncluttered. You have to do the work. There are no shortcuts. And yes, you will face some challenges to make things easier, at least in the short-term. But the end result is

Organizing Tip

Please know that I am not just throwing out positive affirmations as if these will set you on the path to living a more balanced and joyful life. Some people find affirmations really helpful—again, you do you. The work, and the challenge, is real. I am not more immune to it than you are. I have to continually work and tweak my own systems to stay organized and balanced. In the end, we can push against the changes we need to make and resist moving forward, or we can choose ease and grace and grow.

priceless. You'll find that you have more space, more time, and more joy in your life when you declutter, physically, emotionally, and psychologically.

Most clients come to me after years of stress, frustration, and unhappiness with their space and their lives. They want something different; they just aren't sure what *it* is or how to find it. *It* always involves change. Change in what you keep in your space. Change in how you view your space and your life in totality. Change in how you care for yourself from a wholeness and wellness perspective. But getting started on that change can be difficult, even very difficult. If you have decided to focus on financial stability and growth, you might hire a financial planner or accountant to help you. Many people starting on a wellness and fitness journey join a gym or hire a personal trainer. If you need help with starting on an organizing project, hire a professional organizer or organizing coach. We all need support and guidance; it's a sign of strength, not weakness, to admit you need help.

Organizing Tip

Organizing is a process, not an event. This is just the start of your organizing, not the end. Like with fitness, organizing is a journey, not a destination.

I hope you are reading this book with the understanding that living a life of balance is the goal. But if you need that quick "pick me up" and motivator, try jump starting your organization to see how impactful it feels. These are some quick tips to get started on an organizing project from my blog. I like to think of them as *Seven Steps to Get to Your Happy Place.*

1. Start in the kitchen, bedroom, playroom—whichever room feels most impactful for you. Go back to the exercise about finding your pain point. What area causes you the most stress and frustration on a daily basis? Clients often want to jump into attic and basement space when the mudroom is overflowing with clutter and they've worn the same ten items in their wardrobe for the past month. Save the bigger projects for when you have more time (and support and guidance).

2. Set the timer on your phone for sixty minutes and get started. You will need a minimum of sixty minutes to do a "sweep" and then another few minutes to put everything into its proper space. I love that clients want to be ambitious and forge ahead with organizing projects. But putting "time and space" parameters around your organizing session keeps it from feeling overwhelming. With sixty minutes to start, you're forced to stay focused on one particular area.

3. Stand in the entryway and look to your left. Are there items that jump out as clutter? Clutter is anything that is not in its proper "home" or is unneeded. Continue to work your way around the space, starting with anything in the open and then moving into closed storage spaces. Beware! When opening a closet, drawer, or cabinet, you may feel overwhelmed by what you find inside. That's okay. Start with anything that jumps out as not belonging—i.e. Legos in the laundry room or tennis balls in the kitchen. Start with the obvious and take a solid first pass at

the clutter. Another good starting point is anything on the floor that's making walking around the space a hazard. "Safety first" is a great organizing rule.

4. Should the Harry Potter books remain in the family room but not on top of the Xbox? Start here. Take a few items from the top of the pile and relocate them to their proper location in the room. Is the proper "home" the bedroom, the basement, or another space? Use a bin or laundry basket to contain the items that need to go. Gather and containerize the items this way so you don't spend time walking back and forth. Stay in the space until the timer sounds! We waste so much time and energy walking one item up to the bedroom and then something else into the garage. Wait and do this at the end.

5. Is the item you're holding worth keeping? Should it be relocated or is it something that you can do without? Not sure how to decide? Run it through the filter of "usefulness and joy." Is the item useful and needed in your home? Keep it and decide where it should be "housed." Does it bring you joy when you look at it? Keep it—everyone needs beautiful and joyful things in their home. Can't remember the last time you used the item or why you have it? Let it go. Put all your donations into one pile.

6. When the timer goes off, stop organizing. Go through your bin and put away the items to be relocated and put your donations in your car to be dropped off at the nearest donation center. And please, don't get hung up on where to donate the items you are parting

with. If you have something specific to donate, do it immediately. We all want to feel that the things that we've loved and used will be appreciated and used by others. But I've seen many clients get hung up on finding "just the right place to donate this to" and it never gets done. There's a way to donate almost anything—learn more at Where to Donate Anything in the appendix.

7. Congratulate yourself on starting this process. But organizing is a process, not an event. Book a time for another appointment with yourself and keep going! Your clutter did not build up in a day and you will not declutter in a day. Be proud of what you've started and keep up the momentum. Do you see why reading this book and working with an organizing coach is so valuable? Professional organizers and organizing coaches help you define your goal, work hand in hand with you on implementation, keep you motivated, and celebrate your successes.

Finding more space and more time are the two most common challenges for most of us. How do I find space for the things I really need and love? How do I open psychological space in my head and quiet all the noise? In addition to more space, finding and creating more time is a very common organizing goal. So how do I find space and time in my life? You find more space, more time, and more joy by letting go of the stuff that's holding you down and holding you back. All of this includes stuff we've purchased, stuff we've been gifted, stuff we don't need or use—it all takes up physical and psychic space. Caring for our stuff takes up a lot of time as well. Repairs, upkeep, moving and storing our stuff is time-consuming. Purging our unwanted and unneeded items frees up time to do things we really want to do.

Joy and happiness are not something that we can purchase or find; happiness is not out "there." We find joy when we are truly in the moment and doing something we enjoy. In a space overcrowded with unneeded and unused items, we cannot find joy in our space. If we're spending our time and money buying, fixing, maintaining, and trying to find our stuff, we lose time that could be better spent doing something we love. Instead of putting things on your bucket list for someday, make today the day you start to do those things. If you're not rushing around trying to find your car keys, you can listen to a great podcast. Dust off the art project that got put aside. Aim for more down dog and less chaos.

Your space and financial, physical, and emotional health reflect your inner life and inner health. Our "outer life" is a direct reflection of our thinking. My thinking reflects how content I am. How fulfilled I am. How loving I am. My space is the outward expression of what I value, what I enjoy, and what's important to me. Similarly, how you spend money and manage it mirrors how you value and respect yourself and your loved ones. In the words of the indomitable Aretha Franklin: R-E-S-P-E-C-T yourself!

Getting organized helps you make better choices in your spending and your life. Everyone, including organizers, has that space in their home or office that's an organizing challenge. My friend Amy has a spare room she calls her "room of shame." Does your mudroom/transitional space get messy and cluttered quickly and repeatedly? It's often a struggle to keep basements organized. That large open space becomes a dumping ground for things we don't quite know what to do with. Is the playroom with all the kids' games and activities filled with overflowing bins? Despite abundant storage, are items still covering the floor? Most people can point out quickly what space is not working for them. Conversely, most everyone has a space that does work well. The pantry is uncluttered, food items are containerized, and the space works for everyone in the family. Your closet and wardrobe are easy to negotiate and you can find a great outfit quickly and easily. The office has an organized filing system that makes it simple to find your documents when you need them. So, what works for you?

I ask clients about the space that works because it will give us good ideas on how to create more of it. We set up a good working closet and wardrobe by purging the unneeded clothes and accessories. This makes the remaining items easy to see and choose from which simplifies getting dressed. Can we use this same method in the basement? Purge the unneeded and unused items and find an appropriate home for what needs to stay. Great work setting up an office that makes you more efficient and minimizes stress. What similar systems can you create in the mudroom to deal with the volume and variety of items that fill that space regularly?

Everyone has a space that challenges them but at the same time, everyone has a space or system that works well. Look at the processes and systems that are working well and be proud of that. By replicating these successful systems in your challenging spaces, you'll be able to create more space that works.

22

Honoring
Your Legacy

*"We don't attach to things; we attach
to our stories about things."*

—**Byron Katie**

In my work, I have done offices, warehouses, storage units, home offices, basements, garages, sheds, and room after room after room. I have managed technology installations, moves, business planning, personal planning, and multiple projects. While there have definitely been struggles and challenges for my clients along the way, the greatest challenge I have seen, across the board, is memorabilia. Why is it that we can manage a move across the country, or to another country, but we cannot organize memorabilia?

Do you have a box, bin, or closet full of memorabilia that just sits there, hidden away, gathering dust and potentially degrading by the day? Let yourself off the hook on this one.

You are like most people with "stuff" they just don't know what to do with. Photos, documents, clothes, china, furniture, silver; you name it and I've seen it. So, what *is* memorabilia exactly? Webster's Dictionary defines memorabilia as "things that are remarkable and worthy of remembrance." Are all the things you have tucked away "remarkable and worthy of remembrance"? Probably not. Regardless, we hold onto stuff that has memories for us or the people who gifted or left these items to us.

Here's the hard truth: Stuff doesn't hold memories; we imbue it with memories. When we look at Grandma's dishes we remember Sunday dinners when we were children. Holding onto our maternity clothes or our children's baby clothes decades later serves as a memory keeper and placeholder for when we were young, vital, and needed. Seeing Grandpa's pipe reminds us of him and the scent of the pipe tobacco instantly conjures up more memories. This is what is referred to as a visceral memory; it invokes a physical reaction. My grandfather Papere, who lived in Vermont, smoked a pipe. We visited in the summer and that smell *was* him. Almost forty years later, whenever I smell pipe smoke, I instinctively think of my grandfather. That's how memories work and that's what memorabilia can invoke for us. And that's a wonderful thing.

Our memories and legacy are important. Our very nature as humans is to be part of a group, a clan, a pack. Humanity has survived and evolved over thousands of years because of our desire and drive to help each other out; until fairly recently our very survival depended on it. "Next to physical survival, the greatest need of a human being is psychological survival—to be understood, to be affirmed, to be validated, to be appreciated."[11] We use these ties to a previous time and prior generations as a touchstone for our present lives. I would argue that memorabilia are some of the most important things that we keep. These items can be the very nature of things that bring us joy.

So if these things are so important to you, why aren't they out where you can see them and enjoy them? How are you honoring your father's legacy in the armed services by leaving his medals tarnishing in a box hidden away in the basement? If your summers at the lake with your cousins were so important to you, where are the photos? We honor our legacy and our memories by sharing, displaying, and truly treasuring them. Burying them in a box or bin is not honoring a legacy; in fact, it's just the opposite.

Once you have the memorabilia in one spot, set aside significant time to work on this project. (This is a great winter or rainy spring project.) You will not manage or organize your memorabilia in one sitting—it is not humanly possible. Plan

Organizing Tip

As I have told many clients over the years, memorabilia will stop you in your tracks when you are doing a whole house declutter. If you are preparing to move, decluttering a number of spaces, or have a tight timeline for a significant project like a remodel, managing your memorabilia has to take lower priority. Gather all the memorabilia into one spot in the house. Set aside time to come back to the project when you have time to focus on it.

to break the project down into manageable chunks and get started. It helps to define a certain amount of space, i.e. a bin, box, or even a closet, for memorabilia. Once the space is full, you need to review the items and purge what no longer passes muster. If you've decided that this item is important enough to remain and use valuable storage space to keep, why is it hiding? Pull out that box and open that closet—is everything in there "remarkable and worthy of remembrance?" Good; keep it. If not, let it go.

Memorabilia can take many forms—photos, documents, books, clothes, personal items—the list is endless. Photos and documents are actually the easiest to store—I devote the next chapter to this important topic so I can delve into it in more detail. But other memorabilia is definitely harder to manage because of its shape and bulk. For clothes, I understand that parting with "important" and "memorable" items can be challenging. Often clients struggle with anxiety and guilt about getting rid of things like baby clothes or wedding items. Your wedding dress is a thing. It is a symbol of your wedding but it is not the love and partnership and family that you have created through your marriage. No one should feel "bad" about moving that item on. My very clever friend turned her wedding dress into a christening dress for her babies. The reality is that your daughter is unlikely to wear your wedding dress and I expect my sons are definitely not going to have use for mine! If you feel that you just *can't* get rid of it, have it professionally cleaned and preserved and then find an out-of-the-way place to store it. Do not use the prime real estate of your closets for a wedding dress; this is wasted space.

If you're ready to part with your wedding outfit or other

special occasion items, the key to donation is to do it sooner rather than later. Unless an item is professionally cleaned and preserved right after wearing, it's highly likely it will yellow with age. Heat and moisture are common in attics and basements and this is where a lot of clothing "memorabilia" gets stored. Heat especially will accelerate the yellowing process. So those beautiful outfits you put in a bin or box to save for your grandchildren will likely be yellowed, spotted, and unwearable by the time the new grandbaby arrives. If the item is very special, like a christening or bris outfit, preserve it appropriately by keeping it wrapped in conservation paper in a cedar chest or another long-term storage option. Also, moths are attracted to dirt and perspiration. Wash or have your important items professionally cleaned before storing to reduce exposure. I'll talk more about clothing and wardrobe in Chapter 25 of this section: When I Look Good, I Feel Good.

In addition to our special clothing, we have a tendency to hold onto our children's clothing long after they've outgrown it. Why do we do this? Because it reminds us of that special time when our kids were babies and they needed us. Now our teenagers need rides, money, and space away from us. But looking at those tiny booties and outfits fills us with love and incredulity that our cranky and uncommunicative teen was ever that size. Frankly, sometimes parents *really* need that feeling … but space is limited. We can only keep so much. Properly preserve those select items and donate the bulk to someone who can use it now. There are so many groups and organizations within your community that would be grateful for your donations. When you make these donations, think of them as service. We are serving our communities and we are serving ourselves in expressing our gratitude for all we have. In her book, *Growing Whole*, the author Molly Young Brown puts it this way: "Service is the practice of wholeness."

While donating and paying it forward are important and valuable to living a grateful and joyful life, reselling pricier items is an option as well. Online consignment shops for children's and women's clothing have really exploded in the last few years. Reduce, reuse, and recycle. Did you save lots of your child's Little League and youth T-shirts? Guilty on that one! A T-shirt blanket is a wonderful reuse of those items and is a perfect complement to any dorm room. There are lots of online companies that make these, and I chose a local one that employed veterans. I had a blanket made for each of my sons when he went off to college and it remains a prized possession. Why? Because it's the physical reminder of many wonderful memories. Youth sports, school, family trips, time with friends—all encompassed in a blanket. And frankly, getting thirty T-shirts out of the drawer was a huge bonus!

Organizing Tip

Organizing Tip: Find your local craft store. You can buy shadowbox frames and do the work yourself. (I use a glue gun to adhere shirts to the backing.)

Clothing memorabilia can be displayed and treasured in other ways too. When each son completed his high school football "career" and received his jersey, I put the jersey inside a shadow box with photos from each season and other assorted memorabilia. Then up on the wall in the basement it went. Ditto for baseball championship jackets and team jerseys. Shadow boxes are my go-to for memorabilia. The depth and size are perfect for bulkier items. Now when we enter the basement, we can see and enjoy the memories that those many years of sports brought. Why not do the same for dance outfits, martial arts uniforms, or music memorabilia?

> **Caveat: If you can afford it, let the professionals do the work with something as important as a diploma or other special item.**

Memorabilia is an item "worthy of remembrance." Does it still have the same significance today as it did when you tucked it away a decade ago? Go through your items and see if the piece still resonates with you. If so, determine the best way to display it. Remember, space is a finite thing. You may need to think outside the box on how to best display your treasured pieces. Go back and review some of the options from Part 1: More Space on finding the right storage and display space.

Memorabilia projects can be very overwhelming because of the emotion associated with our stuff. Start with these steps to get your arms around the project:

1. Collect memorabilia from all parts of the house and office. Yes, offices have a surprising amount of memorabilia! Sales awards, company historical photos, T-shirts from the company picnic—all of these items fall under the category of memorabilia. This is an opportunity to decide what really is worthy of being saved and what can go. I've seen lots of closets, cabinets, and storage space stuffed with old company tchotchkes, which results in clutter

and mess. If you're clearing out the volume, set up a common area where employees can choose a mug, pen, or sweatshirt from the pile. Leave it there for a week and then donate the remainder.

2. Sort your items by person or event. Are your wedding photos mixed in with your grandmother's baking tools? This is a great place to use plastic bins with lids for bulky items and zip top bags for photos or clothes. Create as many categories as you need so that your items can be separated quickly and easily and then put into the bin or bag. This is a quick sort! This is not the time to ohhh and ahhh over every baby photo or review every document from your grandfather's long-closed law practice. Put the items into the respective categories until everything is separated. Discard any blurry photos or unusable items. By reducing the bulk as you go, you'll end up with more workable categories.

3. What's the story this item tells? In her book *The Growth Mindset*, Carole Dweck reflects on getting to the heart of who we are and what we value. Often this can be about our emotional and spiritual values as well as the *things* we value. "Nothing is better than seeing people find their way to things they value." Unfortunately, time and the elements may have already made the decision on what to keep and what to let go. If anything is falling apart, has mold, or is not in displayable condition, let it go immediately. Photos can be restored with some effort and cost, but if a baby blanket or shawl is stained and yellowed, it

Organizing Tip

Safety first! I have had clients find guns, ammunition, swords, and knives in family memorabilia boxes. Take these items immediately to your local police station for safe disposal. If you want to display great granddad's old revolver or the sword grandpa brought home from the Pacific, be sure these are stored safely inside locked cases.

is beyond repair. If the item is meaningful, prepare to display it. Can't find a good reason to save it? Move it out.

4. Designate an area for display in your home or office. Again, this is an opportunity to make intentional decisions. Group items or photos together so that they tell a story. "Gallery walls" are a good example of this. Bookcases are ideal for those treasured items as well. Decide on the best spot and manner to display the memorabilia—don't just stick it on the shelf and forget about it. If it's remarkable and worthy of remembrance treat it that way.

5. Don't let Mother Nature decide for you. Choose the right storage for your items before they fade or get ruined. In Chapter 9: What Is Good Storage and an Effective System?, I describe some common challenges around storage and choosing the right storage option. I have seen many clients heartbroken over broken china, ruined photos, and yellowed clothing. If an item is important to you but you're not quite

ready or able to display it, take the time to ensure that
it is stored properly for the future.

Different items need different storage solutions and the
options will vary depending on how you want to display
or store them. Photo books? Shadow boxes? Digital photo
frames? Traditional scrapbooks? There are lots of options
available. There are organizers who work specifically in photo
and memorabilia management. If this is an important project
for you, consider working with one of these specialists to get
the project started. Time is not on your side with this project
so the sooner you can get started on this, the better.

But respecting and honoring your legacy by displaying things
you love reflects your true values and brings you joy. Display
your photos and other memorabilia now.

23

So Many Photos!

*"Photography is an art of teleporting
the past into the future."*

—Mehmet Murat ildan

Regardless if you're twenty-three, fifty-three, or seventy-three, welcome to the club of so many photos! Many people have a collection of photos—both printed and digital—that they just don't know what to do with. Because this is such a hot button issue with so many clients, it's important to break down and segment this important topic. Like many organizational issues, how and where we store our photos is critical. As the ease of taking photos has increased exponentially, our "storage" has failed to keep up with the volume. From slides, to negatives and prints, then SD cards, and now cloud storage, the way we store and manage our photos has evolved 180 degrees. And while many of us have moved along with the technology on how photos are taken our organization and storage of prints and digital files has not kept up the pace. To better manage this multifaceted topic, let's start by focusing on print photos that you already have.

I have seen boxes, bins, albums, shoeboxes, envelopes, drawers, and baskets overflowing with photos. These might be print photos you took or older photos that were handed down to you. Some of these might be neatly ensconced in three-ring photo albums, or loose. With print photos, it's critical to store them in a dry, cool place away from excessive heat and moisture. Heat and moisture are the enemies of photos! As with all memorabilia, start by gathering your prints into one place. Open all the drawers, cabinets, and hiding spots for your photos to get your arms around the volume of the printed photos.

Once you have all the photos gathered together, start to create categories. Do a simple sort of "heritage" photos including your family of origin. If you're dealing with dozens instead of hundreds of photos, choose a simple storage solution like a large manila envelope or zip top bag. Clearly label your envelope or bag so you take the guesswork out (ex. "Lisa's Family Photos" or "Roy Family"). Then use smaller envelopes or plastic bags to hold photos of childhood, school, family, etc. in whatever categories that work for you. For this simple sort, use broad categories and don't get bogged down in specifics. Creating too many subcategories is not necessary at this stage and this can be very time-consuming.

Repeat the process with more recent photos, and organize by event, person, or year. Archival photo boxes are great and if having your photos stored in them is helpful for you, go for it.

Organizing Tip

She who organizes the photos decides on what to keep. If you are the legacy keeper for your family or organization and there is a truly unflattering photo of yourself or someone else, get rid of it! You are under no obligation to keep every photo you have—some (many!) are not worthy of keeping. We all have too many photos of the inside of Disney World's "It's a Small World" ride— pare down to a few great photos. If there isn't a person in the photo, get rid of many of the landscape photos. Keep anything that evokes a certain memory and let the others go. Did you find duplicates or a special photo you want to forward and share? Send them with a card or take a photo and share it today.

I don't use them or generally recommend them because most people don't need that level of categorizing and the boxes themselves can be inconvenient. There is nothing easier than slipping a photo inside of a large envelope or storage bag. Remember, this is a "quick sort" to give you basic categories to work with. This is not the time to relive every memory. Be efficient and somewhat ruthless on the quality of the photos. This is also a great time to purge, purge, purge! Throw out the blurry, cut off, and simply "bad" photos.

> **Caveat: Share photos now sparingly. If you know that you won't be getting back to this project for a while, take two minutes now (remember the two minute rule?) and do it today. Did you find a particularly great photo of you and your cousins at the family**

BBQ? Scan it or take a photo with your smartphone and share it with that person directly. I always recommend asking before posting on social media for a photo that includes anyone else. Perhaps that event or time in your friend's life was not particularly happy—so posting anyone else's photo on social media is tricky.

Getting a handle on loose photos and the volume of what you are working with is critical. It helps segment the project into manageable chunks. Congratulate yourself on completing important step one. Rome was not built in a day. Your photo pile was not built in a day either. Let go of the guilt around not completing this project. Baby steps.

If you have photos in the old style albums with sticky pages and plastic covers, remove them immediately. Because the glue on these pages is highly acidic, it is eating away at your photos, which is why they appear yellowed. Do another sort with these photos and put them into the categories you used before.

Organizing Tip

Removing photos from sticky-paged albums is a great project to handle while watching TV or a movie. It's a simple process to remove photos from the sticky-backed pages, but be careful if the photos do not remove easily. Use a butter knife to lift the photo from the backing. If you remove the plastic cover, the pages themselves are usually recyclable.

Use this same sorting process for photos in frames no longer on display. Junk or donate the broken and mismatched frames and save the good and meaningful photos. Once you have all of your photos together, store them in a plastic tub or box away from heat and moisture to protect them.

With this quick sort, try to pare down what you have into the very best photos. Do you have all your photos in broad categories? Be proud of getting this done as this is not an easy project. Creating categories and sorting your photos is an excellent start. It's what Charles Duhigg in his book, *The Power of Habit*, calls a "small win." "Small wins are steady application of a small advantage. Small wins fuel transformative changes by leveraging tiny advantages into patterns that convince people that bigger achievements are within reach."[12]

Okay, I put the photos together—now what? The prints can now be scanned to digital, put into quality photo albums, added to frames—you have lots of options. Are these print photos part of the legacy you are honoring and preserving? If so, what's your goal for your photo memorabilia? Will you make traditional albums? Are you adding special photos to frames around your space? Do you want to create digital photo books? For photo memorabilia management, set a goal for your project. I've done many photo memorabilia projects over the years. Some clients were focused on preserving family history and memories before it was lost for coming generations. Remember, if you are dealing with heritage photos, record the who, what, where, and when of the photos now. If we don't actively save it, information will likely be lost and that part of your history, and legacy, will be gone.

Honoring a Brother's Legacy

I worked on a special project for a client who had lost
a sibling and wanted a better way to remember and
honor his memory. E. and her brother had lived together
in their family home for his entire life. She had so many
wonderful memories of him and was struggling to figure
out how to best organize her photos so she could enjoy
them. They had taken many, many wonderful trips
together over the years so there was a lot of volume
to manage. E.'s goal was to create albums so that she
could go through them and enjoy the memories, but
she struggled with how to do that. There were lots of
photos—hundreds—that chronicled his well-lived life.
She had purchased some albums and started to put the
photos in, but quickly became overwhelmed with the
project and how to move it forward. It was at that point
that she called me.

E. had a defined goal: put the photos in albums to
enjoy and remember—but she did not have a process or
system to make that happen. Together, we sorted all the
photos into the appropriate categories using the quick
sort method. Childhood, school, work, various trips, at
home—these were the categories we used to lay out the
albums. And then we went chronologically, recreating
her brother's life through the photos. Working on this
project was a labor of love, both for me and the client.
At times I felt like a forensic historian, putting all the
pieces of the "puzzle" together. I was thrilled I was able

(continued)

to utilize the products—the albums, paper, and the other scrapbooking supplies she already had purchased. We added narrative and as much additional memorabilia—pins, badges, newspaper clippings, as well as diplomas and citations—as we could. The end result was beautiful and it achieved exactly what she had desired: a loving remembrance.

My client was not a "technology person." For her, there was no value in scanning and digitizing photos for digital frames, photo books, and slideshows. Also, she did not feel the need to preserve the photos for another generation. Because this did not reflect her goal, we focused only on the photo prints and utilizing them in the best way for her, i.e. traditional photo albums.

E. loves her albums. And I love that she gave me the opportunity to serve her brother's memory.

After sorting your photos, a good next step is to digitize before putting them into traditional albums or adding them to frames. Once a photo is digitized, it can be used, reused, and shared easily. Do you need to digitize a substantial number of photos? I recommend using an online digitizing company. There are many, many options for online photo scanning companies. Costs vary depending on a number of factors including size of the photos. For traditional four-by-six photos, these can be run through a scanner and are much more cost efficient to scan. For larger prints like five-by-seven, eight-by-ten and larger, a flat bed scanner is used and it requires more work from a technician and therefore costs more.

Organizing Tip

If creating traditional print photo albums is your goal, there are lots of quality options available. Be sure to use lignin free and acid free paper and supplies. Creative Memories is a leader in this market and sells excellent products. You can also purchase album supplies at your local arts and craft stores. If you are spending the time to create these albums, choose quality and photo-safe products so that these photos are properly preserved.

Depending on how many photos you have to scan, using an at-home scanner is generally not as cost and time effective. As an organizer, I purchased a flatbed scanner and used it to digitize some of my own photos and have done small (very small) projects for clients over the years. There are pros and cons with using an at home scanner versus using a scanning company so here are some highlights:

Pros:

You are always in possession of your photos. For some people, shipping photos and trusting them to the mail and through the process is a big concern. It's often fear of losing the photos that holds many folks back from moving forward with this project. Decide how risk averse you are. If you are reluctant to ship your photos, search for a local company who will do the scanning. I had a client with over a thousand prints, slides, and videotapes to be converted to digital. She was not comfortable mailing these items so we found a local company who could handle the project. Yes, she paid more to have the project completed but in the end, memories are priceless.

You can manage the project and the timeline. If you have an important event coming up and need these digital files ASAP, you can scan the ones you really need for the event quickly. This is a good option for a small number of photos but for a large volume of photos, this can become very time inefficient.

Cons:

Scanning your own photos is very time-consuming. While scanner technology has come a long way in the past few years, it is still time-consuming to scan your own photos. At home scanners (or multifunction printers with scanning capability) require you to edit and save each photo. This is where a lot of the time comes in. Again, if you are working with a very small group of photos, it's manageable but for a bigger volume, it will require a lot more time.

You will need a computer and editing software to edit your photos. At home scanning is a two part process: First is the physical scan, and second is the editing and saving. There are all-in-one scanners that save the digitized photos as a jpeg on an SD card that you can then edit on your computer. This is a great option if Nana has the only copies of family photos and she will not allow these to leave her home. You can work in place with the photos and scanner and enjoy a cup of tea and some "Nana time" as you scan the precious prints. The speed of the scanning will vary depending on the resolution you choose; the higher the resolution, the slower the scan.

Digitized photos can take up a lot of computer storage space. Remember when you got your first home computer? And then your second and third? New systems always seem to run so fast but after a year or two, they seem to run slower. Is the processing speed slowing down? Nope, that's not it. It's that we've bogged down our systems with applications and files, especially photo files which take up a lot of space. Look back to Chapter 13, How Do I Prioritize My Time with Better Systems? where I talk about how we care for our technology and redundancy.

Once you have your original print photos and digital photo files—whether you scan yourself or outsource this project— you're ready to move on. How can I use my print and digitized photos? In the words of Elizabeth Barrett Browning, "Let me count the ways...."

Use those prints in traditional photo frames and collages. Display your memories! Put photos of special people and occasions out to be enjoyed today. If these photos represent your legacy, you honor that legacy by displaying it, not hiding it away. Some people enjoy creating traditional photo albums; there are many groups and communities focused on this fun activity. For a number of years, I created traditional photo albums using Creative Memories products and have nearly twenty very large albums. I also created legacy albums for my mother and mother-in-law using their family photos. When my boys were little, they loved sitting on the floor and looking through "their" albums. The volume of photos has slowed dramatically with my sons as young adults, but I still add important events to the albums every few months. Why? Because this is our family legacy to share with future generations.

Traditional photo albums and scrapbooking are not for everyone. Are you looking for a less labor intensive project? Quickly create books with your digital photo files. There are many companies that can quickly and easily create this product for you. I've had success with Snapfish and Shutterfly and if you are a MAC user, Apple has software to create a digital photo book as well. One of my favorite options for digital photo files is a digital photo frame. This is a particularly great option for a smaller space, like an elder's apartment or an office.

Once or twice a year, remove the storage device, add more photos and then re-insert and you have new, updated photos to share. All of these options allow you to enjoy your photos today. Taking the time to digitize your photo prints is a very worthwhile, although time consuming, project. While great, print photo uses are limited so digitizing the originals multiplies the value exponentially. Once an image is digitized, you can use it repeatedly; or as they say in marketing "repurpose the content." Then share these photos with others through social media and photo sharing sites and double their impact. Share and enjoy your memories today.

Organizing Tip

For a digital photo frame, I recommend loading photo files onto a USB drive or SD card and then inserting it into the digital photo frame. While most frames state that they hold thousands of photos, that's deceiving. If your photos are higher resolution, which they likely are, you can use a much higher storage option like the USB or SD card and therefore load more photos.

24

Clutter Holds You Back

"Just where you are—that's the place to start."

—**Pema Chodron**

hen I know where to find the things I'm looking for and can fit paper into a file or a towel on a shelf, I have a sense of being more in control of my life. Lunchboxes handy to fill? Backpacks on hand and study supplies out to make homework less stressful? Is my desk clear so I can work on my project? Can I easily pick a great outfit out of my closet for a big meeting? Are my keys hanging by the door so I can "grab and go" to get out the door without frustration? These are the little, but important, things that make our daily lives easier. Eliminating clutter makes the burden of daily life feel lighter when we're not hunting for the things we need. Everyday life—especially with kids—will never be easy, but it can be a whole lot easier. Organization is not the goal.

Joy is the goal. Purposefulness is the goal. Intention is the goal. Organization just makes those other, much more important goals, easier to reach by decreasing and eliminating stress and frustration.

No one should feel stressed when she opens the door to her home. Is your space providing you with a place of peace and calm, of focus and motivation? Or is it a major source of stress and anxiety in your life? Clutter in your home translates to more stress and this leads to our life being out of balance. What's going on in your physical space is a direct reflection of what is going on in your mind. Your outer life reflects your thinking. This is why I call clutter "deferred decisions." You don't know what to do with something, so you just put it down to "deal with it later"; hence clutter. Being surrounded by clutter does not make us feel peaceful; the effect is just the opposite. "Surrounded by a million choices, we are freed from the constraints of need and yet at the same time, challenged to find our focus and meaning in life."[13] All of that clutter was a choice that we made to bring something into our space and leave it there. We have to own our responsibility for our decision to do that.

Have you ever tried to think and plan in a cluttered space? For most of us, that's difficult to do. I've seen clients abandon offices, entire rooms, and even homes because they could no longer face the clutter. We utilize the "dump and run" method. We feel so overwhelmed by our cluttered space that we drop one more thing into that already cluttered space and then flee, unable to even bear being in the space. And the clutter grows and grows. And it starts to creep and take over, like kudzu vines, into your relationships, your work, your wellness, and your life. You move away from living your best life to living a life of overwhelm and mediocrity. Tim Ferriss, the author and speaker, was clear on this. "It's lonely at the top. Ninety-nine percent of people in the world are *convinced* they can't do great things, so they aim for mediocre." The emphasis here is mine, not Tim's. Because I have seen over and over again that clients are convinced that things cannot get better; that they cannot get and stay organized; that they cannot change their habits and behaviors. But I am happy to report that yes, all of that can change. What drives that change? Intention and action. In his excellent book, *The Charge: Activating the 10 Human Drives that Make You Feel Alive*, the author Brendon Burchard puts it this way: "Intentions are not enough; our actions define who we truly are." Organizing systems are great intentions; working and maintaining that organization is an action.

In my practice, I have worked with many families who struggle to function with high levels of clutter and disorganization. It's important to note that children can be influenced by the state of their physical space just as you are. If clutter

Organizing Tip

Start to redefine your definition of clutter. Webster's Dictionary defines clutter as, "a crowded or confused mass or collection." This is a great starting point. Take this definition of "crowded or confused mass" and apply it to thoughts and feelings; emotional and psychological clutter. Anything that does not lift you up in life is holding you down and back.

and disorganization in your home have you feeling frazzled and stressed, it's highly likely that your children will feel this as well. Clutter leads to an environment of overstimulation in the home. Children need activities and toys and they also need calm, uncluttered space for schoolwork, playing, and sleeping. While we talk about the kindergarten model for children's spaces a lot, the same methodology can be used to organize any space.

Organizing Tip

Outgrown car seats and baby tubs are not memorabilia. Put these items into long-term storage spaces like the attic or basement if you feel they will be used in your home again within the next few years. If you feel that your family is complete, pass these items on immediately. Let go of the clutter to make room for what your child now needs—space for learning and development.

In the master bedroom, set up a reading and meditation space with books and good lighting. Carve out a dressing area so that getting dressed each day goes more smoothly. Display photos and other memorabilia in an intentional manner so that the space is even more enjoyable. Decorators and designers use this concept all the time by using furniture and accents to differentiate and segment multiple uses of one space.

Having littles in your space is an organizing challenge; there's no denying that truth. With littles come lots of stuff. Baby stuff, safety stuff, clothes, toys, and … well, just stuff. At some point, we need all of those gifts and purchases. But as the saying goes,

"The days are long and the years are short." All of a sudden your newborn is walking around and those early months and years have gone by in the blink of an eye. So what did you do with all the newborn stuff? Is it still crowding the nursery drawers and closets? That's clutter. Clutter is anything that has no purpose in a space today. If you are holding onto items for sentimental reasons, it has become memorabilia and you should treat it as such.

When children are young, their minds are like sponges; they absorb everything. Because of children's capacity to learn and adapt at this age, it's a great time to create organizing systems. With pre-readers, put pictures or photos on the outside of bins so choosing toys and games is easy. If there's a system for selecting toys, there's also a system for cleaning up and putting away. A neatly organized space for a child to play and learn is key. Children have an amazing capacity for growth if we give them space to do that. A child in a cluttered and messy play-room becomes overstimulated and unable to play and entertain him or herself. There is so much volume and mess he or she cannot decide what to do next and moves chaotically from one activity to the next and the space becomes more cluttered by the day. Have you ever seen a child migrate their toys from the playroom to other areas of the home? That's often because that space is so overwhelming and cluttered it becomes less likely to be used.

Yes, I know that it's time-consuming and tedious to orga-nize children's play spaces. Still, make the time to do a major purge every few months of your child's toys and clothes. In a home with several children, it will absolutely be longer before you can get rid of some items if you have younger children who will soon use those items. But be realistic. The volume of clothes and toys many American children have is staggering. Do a sweep through and get rid of the broken, mismatched, and unusable items. Donate anything that is still usable and trash the rest. Less really is more. Don't believe me? Watch children ignore the expensive toy that came in the big box as they play with the box for hours.

Yes, children's belongings are a huge opportunity for clutter. (I'm talking to you, Shopkins.) But it's difficult to be intentional and help eliminate clutter for others if we struggle to limit our own clutter. A major clutter culprit? Books. And more books. And still more books. I have seen bookcases that are literally collapsing under the weight of the books. I have seen piles and piles of books on the floor, on tables, on chairs, and pretty much every other flat surface.

I love to read; it's one of my very favorite activities. I make reading a part of my daily ritual and I start my day with it. So I understand and connect with book lovers on the joy that comes from reading. But are you actually reading those books? If you have hundreds and hundreds of books, how do you find the time to read them all? The honest answer is that you're not reading all those books. Some of those books you loved and just "cannot part with." Others you intend to read but just haven't quite found the time yet. Other books were given to you and you cannot let them go because they were a gift. And while I like to think of time as boundless and open, most of us don't have all day to sit and read for weeks or months at a time. Because that's how much time you will need to read all of the books you already have in your space. Again, be realistic. Space is finite. Just because we can do something doesn't mean that we should. Just because I *can* fit 270 books on my bookshelves doesn't mean that I *should*. Because that's a lot of books.

In addition to books, tools are another category that grows easily into excessive volume and clutter. Hardware tools like hammers, screwdrivers, nails, and the like seem to multiply overnight. Exactly how many Phillips-head screwdrivers does one home need? Probably no more than two of differing sizes; so how come we have eight? For anyone who is doing restoration or works in the construction trade there will obviously be more tools as this is an occupational requirement. But for most of us, a circular saw is a safety hazard. Like other forms of clutter, tools accumulate and increase because we

Organizing Tip

While I'm a tactile person and love the "feel" of a book, I read 90 percent of books on my e-Reader. It's portable and eliminates the space of the book itself—you can get hundreds of books on an e-Reader. When I'm traveling or on vacation, I load my reader with books, grab my charger and save weight and space in my carry-on. If you're struggling to find more reading time in your busy day, audio books are awesome. I load them on my phone and play them through the audio system in my car. While working in the yard or around the house, I tuck my phone into a pocket and use my headphones. If you love reading, you can find creative ways to engage in this activity. If you love books, how they look and how they feel, that's something different.

forget what we already own or feel the need to buy the special or custom tool because of the "cool" factor. I have seen lots of garages and created a lot of organizing systems in these critical spaces. And most garages and basements have lots of unused and often misplaced items.

In some homes, clutter comes in the form of arts and craft supplies. Some clients have had entire rooms dedicated to art and art projects. These arts and craft tools frequently become clutter because a devotee or artist views the supplies as a necessity, not a luxury. So we keep buying more paints, yarn, fabric, brushes, patterns, thread; you name it and someone has a room full of it. If quilting or painting brings you joy, do more of it. If you lose all track of time when you are scrapbooking or beading, find time for it. The activity itself is not the issue. It's our purchasing and repurchasing of the tools and supplies that leads to clutter. Again, clutter is "a crowded or confused mass or collection." How much yarn is enough? How many paintbrushes can you use? When organizing art and crafting supplies, clients often end up purging 60 to 70 percent of their stock because they know, in the end, they just don't have the time to use it all.

The same principle holds true for cooking and baking tools, office supplies, exercise equipment; there are so many categories that can become clutter in your space. Organization is finding your stuff when you need it. You need one three-hole punch, not three. You need three cookies sheets, not seven. You need one cardio machine, not two. If something has no purpose in your space today or the foreseeable future, remove it. Donate it, put it into longer term storage or recycle it; this is clutter.

Stepping back from our stuff allows us to "see" ourselves more clearly. Our consumer culture tells us to buy, buy, buy to create the life we want. But what if we looked at it differently? What if you can see the life you want by taking away "stuff" from your life? Sometimes it's more of a process of removing layers of stuff to get to the essence of what *is*. Call it the Michelangelo effect. As the sculptor said, "I saw the angel in the marble and carved until I set him free." Where is the angel in your life hiding?

25

When I Look Good, I Feel Good

"Fashion fades, only style remains the same."

—Coco Chanel

My favorite organizing projects, hands down, are wardrobes and closets. I have seen many instances where this is a major sticking point for a client (even though this may not seem obvious in the beginning). Because when I look good, I feel good. Period. And this is hardly limited to my female clients. I have worked with male clients with extensive wardrobes and the issues are the same across the board.

For many people, our closets and drawers are full of clothes we can't easily access or don't fit us, so we don't wear them. Our closets are bulging with unworn and unneeded items.

Organizing Tip

Everyone deserves
to feel good. By
the very nature of
your existence, you
deserve the best in
life. The only clothes
you should have
in your closet are
items that make you
look and feel your
best. Because you
deserve it. If you put
something on, look
in the mirror and
think "Meh. I look
okay." Or "Fine." Or
"Whatever." No. You
deserve better than
that.

Our drawers are so full that oftentimes we can't close them. Wardrobe overflows onto chairs, floors, laundry baskets, and bins, and every flat surface we can find. Is it because we have so many great options that delight us and make us feel our best? Nope. We wear the same outfits over and over again because we just can't get to the rest or it's what we feel comfortable in so we keep repeating the same outfits over and over. According to a survey done by the closet gurus California Closets, we wear 20 percent of our clothes 80 percent of the time. Yes, if you wear a suit, dress shirt, and tie to work, that comprises a lot of that 20 percent. In addition to our work "uniform," in our personal time we also tend to recreate the same outfit over and over.

Before we delve further into the subject of clothes, a note on jewelry (and yes this applies to gentlemen as well as ladies). When working with a client, I always ask, "How do you want to live?" and "How do you envision your space?" The answers to these questions help me hone in on a client's pain point and allow us to create workable solutions. It's quite common for a client to answer that they would love to get dressed with less stress and be able to wear their jewelry. The thing that's stopping them from doing that? The jewelry is in a jumble, hidden away in a drawer or box, unworn. The antidote for that is to find a way to better see and display your jewelry. Beautiful and special things are made to be worn and enjoyed, not hidden away and wasted.

Pick a storage option that allows you to see and choose your jewelry easily. On my website www.yourorganizedlife.biz, I have a how-to video on creating a jewelry display board. I use a simple cork board mounted on my bedroom wall for my "signature" jewelry. This allows me to see everything and pick out what works best for my outfit. Earrings, bracelets, and more delicate necklaces live in a traditional jewelry box on my bureau. Pinterest is a great resource for more options on this. Take the time to organize your jewelry. Get rid of the unmatched earrings, broken items, and stuff you just don't want to wear anymore. Most jewelers will buy back your quality jewelry; if you don't have a relationship with a local jeweler, ask a friend for a recommendation.

For most of us, it's easy to fall into a wardrobe rut. So, let's talk about how to get out of that rut. Again, most people wear 20 percent of their clothes 80 percent of the time. Think back to what you wore in the past seven days. Was it the same outfit, over and over, with little variation? Was it the black pants with the white top? Or maybe the beige top? The grey suit with the white shirt? Or the blue shirt? Did you choose it because it looks great on you? Or because it was clean and in front of you? Do you think the best that you deserve is a black-and-beige life? Again, if you're in a profession that requires a uniform, you will be wearing the same items consistently.

That's a requirement of your work. But there are many ways to present your own unique, authentic self to the world with small, important details.

How we dress and present ourselves to the world projects how we value ourselves. This is not about being vain or superficial; this is about self-care and self-love. Through our wardrobe, we project our personality and our authenticity to the world and that's a good thing. Think about a friend or acquaintance whose style you admire. Don't copy them; emulate them. As Dolly Parton said, "Figure out who you are and then do it on purpose." It's not about being trendy and buying the latest fashions; it's about being comfortable and authentic in who we are and sharing that.

So, What Should We Get Dad for Father's Day?

One of my favorite clients is a dermatologist. Being in the medical profession doesn't allow for a lot of opportunity to express his personality—so J. does it with his tie collection. And it is extensive. But here's the difference between "clothes clutter" and a true collection; he actually wears the ties. When we were working on streamlining his wardrobe, he did a great job of purging the ties he didn't wear and keeping the ones he loved and wore. Many of these had been gifts over the years—remember all of those Father's Day presents? With an amazing memory, he could remember when the kids, now grown and married, had given them and so they had sentimental value. And

(continued)

yet, he was amazing about realizing that we just can't keep everything. When everything has value, nothing has value.

Knowing that the tie collection would be a challenge, both from a volume and sentimentality perspective, we kept that project until the end. Instead, we started with the "easy" items: the worn-out workout gear, too big pants, the unworn shirts. Going drawer by drawer and shelf by shelf, we cleared out what J. wasn't wearing. At the same time, we started a shopping list for the few items to add so he could shop selectively for those items that would have the greatest impact. (When starting a large organizing project like this, I generally recommend starting with the "easy" stuff. Decision-making builds. If you can start by gathering momentum with easier decisions, you'll stay motivated and moving forward with the bigger, more challenging decisions.)

To make purging the volume of the ties easier, I put them into broad categories: animals, holiday, vocational, etc. By doing this, J. was able to go through them as a group, deciding how many ties with dogs he really wanted to keep. Viewing them as a category within his wardrobe makes that decision easier, winnowing down into manageable chunks.

J. totally rocks his ties ...

One of the reasons we tend to wear the same items over and over is that these items are front and center. They might be fresh out of the wash or on top in the drawer and we just can't be bothered to dig down and find something different. For many of us, our wardrobe blahs are a result of poor closet management. Closet organization is an important first step in creating a wardrobe that makes you feel vibrant and good about you; this is a very worthwhile goal. When we feel good about how we look, there's an extra bounce in our step. We are happier and more outgoing. We feel confident and relaxed in our "big meeting" attire and contribute at a higher level. We smile more and the world smiles back. Forget what your mom told you about saving items for that "special occasion." Today is that special occasion. Wear the pretty dress. Put on the jewelry. Pick out a fun and funky tie. You'll be amazed at the reaction you get, both internal and external.

Creating a fun and functional wardrobe starts with purging those items that just don't work for us. Cutting the wheat from the chaff allows you to start with what works and create a wardrobe system from there. Again, this is a process that will require you to make it worse before you can make it better. This project will take a number of hours, especially if you have an extensive wardrobe and lots of items you haven't worn in a while. Plan accordingly!

Organizing Tip

If closets and drawers are overflowing for all your family members, start with the kids' rooms. Because children grow so quickly, eliminating what's too small, too stained, or too tired-looking should be a quick process. Purge, purge, purge. If items are in the process of being passed down, set a time frame of six months. If Sally's clothes won't fit Tammy for another year or so, move it out into alternate, long-term storage space so what Tammy needs for today fits in the space. Ready to move out Tammy baby clothes? Keep one or two of the most special outfits and donate the rest.

Once the kids' clothes are better organized, focus on your wardrobe. Your ability to get dressed and out the door feeling ready for the day is huge. It sets you up for success in your day in a small but important way.

> **Caveat:** Here's a good place to remind readers (and listeners) that I am a parent and I have always worked outside the home. I've been told by colleagues that I have baby puke down the back of my shirt. I have worn yoga pants for more days in a row than I would care to admit. I know how difficult it is to take just five minutes from a hectic morning schedule to focus on what I'm wearing. I know that no one else really cares what I look like when I drop my kids off at school and then run to the grocery store. My messy bun and oversized shirt aren't a "big deal." But I should care. Because not paying attention to myself sets me up for other neglectful decisions. The attitude of, "I'm just a mom and how I look isn't important," sends a negative message about how you value yourself. It also sets a lousy example of self-care and self-love to your children. If you're wearing jeans and a sweater and you get a lot of "My! Why are you so dressed up?" comments, take heed—you need to up your wardrobe game.

Get real about why you haven't focused on your wardrobe before and commit to changing your habits. Eleanor Roosevelt said, "Always do what you are afraid to do." Today, that thing might be excavating the back of your closet. Again, this is a task that really benefits from working with a professional organizer or organizing coach. Often, we are not the best judge of what looks good on ourselves and we tend to fall back into the "okay," "fine," or, "it'll do" rut. This is a place where we need to be pushed out of our comfort zone. Or as Emerson stated, "Our chief want in life is somebody who shall make us do what we can." Purging and organizing my closet can quickly overwhelm and paralyze; get the support you need to keep going. This is a project that really requires us to be nonjudgmental, kind and loving with ourselves. I have worked with clients who are angry and disappointed in themselves for spending money on clothes that don't fit or they don't need. These feelings can cause this project to go awry quickly.

If you have been neglectful in this area, this project can feel very daunting. I have had clients with full walk-in closets and entire rooms full of clothes and accessories. One of the reasons we ignore this project is that maybe we've changed sizes and we know that many of our clothes just don't fit right now. Stop beating yourself up. We all change sizes—accept it

Organizing Tip

Only enlist a friend or family member whose style you admire if you absolutely feel that person can be supportive and noncritical. Your support person, ideally a professional, will keep you focused and motivated. A partner in believing will give you unbiased opinions on what to keep and what should go. "Gentle in what you do. Firm in how you do it," as Buck Brannaman, the horse whisperer, would say. Having a critical "helper" with this work, or any organizing project, will make the process much more challenging.

and move on. Organizing your wardrobe is not for the faint of heart; that's why many people never take on this task. Another reason this important task goes unaddressed is that clients feel that they don't have the money to go out and purchase a whole new wardrobe. I never have seen this happen in all my years of organizing. When the project is complete, reward yourself with a few new purchases to fill some gaps in your wardrobe. When you manage your wardrobe in this way, your new purchases are doubly impactful and enjoyable.

Set aside a few hours for the task—this is a great rainy day project. Grab some large trash bags and laundry baskets. Create a good working surface by clearing and making the bed so you can lay things out. Take a deep breath. Here are some steps to get started:

Gather clothes and accessories from other parts of the house if they are scattered around. You don't have to grab the clean laundry and add it to the pile; that's a job for after you've organized your drawers and closet. (If the clothes are clean or in the laundry, you already know you're wearing it.) If you leave certain items in your transitional space—i.e. your gym bag or everyday jackets—leave them there. Again, you already know you wear them and don't need to make decisions about them. If these items are in good shape and are working for you, leave them be. However, if any of these items are tired and ratty-looking and you need to make better decisions about them, add them to the project.

Start from the bottom up and tackle everything on the floor. In a rush, we tend to dump items on the floor figuring we'll get to them later. But when "later" never comes, items continue to pile up and we can't find what we need when we need it. Shoes, purses, shopping bags, and items that have fallen often cover the bottom of closets. Pull everything out; yes, everything. You have to know what you have in order to decide what stays and what goes. If your wardrobe is spilling out onto the floor of the bedroom, include that space as part of the closet. You need to create a working space so starting on the floor gives you space to work. Starting from the bottom up will give you room to move around instead of tripping over items strewn around the floor.

Create categories. When I work with clients, I use several large bins and extra large trash bags. Immediately create a donate bag. This will likely be your largest category! If you do a regular closet overhaul, there should be less to donate, but for most of us, we'll find many items that can go. Use a bin or laundry basket for your "try on" pile. Again, this may be a large category for you if you haven't seen some of these items in months or even years. This is a critical step that you should not skip! If you haven't worn something in a significant length of time, there's likely a reason for it (in addition to your not having seen it). Is it not a good fit? Is the color or shape not ideal for you? Is the repair work not worth the cost of the garment?

> **Caveat: Don't waste money and time on repairing or cleaning items you are questioning keeping; try those items on prior to mending or cleaning. There will also be a fairly large laundering category; clients love tossing these items into a pile to be dealt with later.**

Purge, purge, and purge some more! Remove the stuff you really don't love or need and donate or consign it. It does you no good sitting in your closet taking up valuable real estate. You will absolutely find items you stopped wearing for the simple reason that you forgot they were there. These are gems! In the organizing world, we call this "shopping your closet"— consider this a bonus! Anything you are ambivalent about, put in the "try on" pile.

When we start this project, clients tend to be hesitant about purging items, feeling they will have nothing left to wear. Here's the reality: You've been wearing a fraction of your wardrobe all along. If you haven't touched, worn, or missed an item in months or years, you are unlikely to miss it if it goes. Not sure? Put it in the try on pile. Once you try it on, you might "remember" why you stopped wearing it in the first place.

Move some items to longer-term storage. The goal of good closet management is to be able to quickly and easily find a great outfit to wear on a daily basis. Some items will fall into the "special occasion" category like fancy dresses and suits or seasonal items. If possible, move these items to other storage areas in the home. I hang our "party" wear in the guest room closet because the bedroom closet, which I share with my husband, is pretty small. The key is to keep these like items together and not scatter them all over. We both know that dressy clothes are in the guest room closet so we know to go there when we are looking for them. Segment out the space in your closet so your everyday items are front and center, and use the back of the closet for seldom-used items. How is the tux hanging front and center in your closet helping you get out the door every day? Unless you are a professional emcee, it's not. Go back and review Part I: More Space for ideas on creating zones and using alternate storage spaces to open up your everyday and most highly trafficked spaces.

Create a "Not Today" space. Here is another great opportunity to be honest and realistic. Sizing is all over the place, especially with women's clothing. If the numbers are significantly different than the sizes you are currently wearing, either purge them or create your "Not Today" space. I have worked with many clients who get really down on themselves about their weight and clothes that no longer fit. This is self-defeating and unkind. Be conscious of your language and don't berate yourself for being at a different weight and unable to wear the dress from college. I categorize these items as "not working for me right now." Put these items, if they are in good condition and still stylish, into the Not Today category and find some alternate space to store them. Focus on the garment itself, not the size. If you can fit into that item at some point, is it still a good option for you? If the answer is no, then donate or consign it today.

Once you've purged your wardrobe and determined what needs to go and what's staying, take some time to plan out how to set up your closet for maximum success. Please don't skip this process and just shove everything back in. Creating an effective closet organization can be hugely impactful. Again, it's about how the space can work best for you.

Make sure you have proper lighting. Can you see into the back corners of your closet where clothes are lurking? If you don't have existing lighting in the closet, add battery operated tap lights. You can't wear what you cannot see. And all of that darkness is depressing. Some clever clients repaint the inside of closets a bright and cheery color. What a wonderful

Organizing Tip

I have had clients tell me that they keep differently sized clothing in the closet as motivation for change. You do you. If the visual of the dress or suit hanging there motivates you to eat healthier and work out more, by all means leave it there. For most of us, however, this is un-motivating. Seeing clothes that don't work for us clutter up our closet can lead to a lack of enthusiasm for getting dressed. We end up in the ho-hum of "good enough." If this has been a struggle for you, create healthy habits and routines that motivate you instead of showcasing the actual garment. Everyone deserves to feel beautiful every day regardless of size or shape. We are all on a journey to our best selves—why not look great on that journey?

way to make getting dressed more fun each day. If trying to find something to wear on a rainy Monday morning feels like entering the catacombs beneath Rome, know this is not setting you up for success.

Pull out empty hangers! Empty hangers take up a lot of room; they make pulling items out difficult if they are caught up with empty ones. Take your wire hangers on your next run to the dry cleaner—they will recycle and reuse them. Metal hangers are fine for dress shirts and blouses but that's it. Many women's blouses in non-cotton materials slide and fall off the wire hangers, and heavier items literally bend the hangers and clothes end up misshapen. Invest in quality hangers—this is a good splurge. My personal favorites are the huggable, slimline velvet hangers. Some clients prefer

Organizing Tip

Back in Chapter 5: Making Transitional Space Work, I talked about closet management for coats. I strongly recommend quality wooden hangers for heavy coats. I have seen wire hangers collapsing under the weight of an overcoat. Using ineffective solutions like this makes accessing our stuff time-consuming and more difficult. Purchase some solid wooden or plastic/acrylic hangers for heavy items; it is well worth the investment. You can get these at any Target or Bed Bath Beyond locations and online.

plastic or acrylic options; use whatever feels best for you. The goal is to be able to see and access items in your closet so that you can quickly pick a great outfit and get out the door.

Before returning clothes to the closet, I suggest removing dry cleaning plastic immediately. This plastic covering is not intended for long-term storage. Dry cleaning requires chemicals (even the green versions) to clean your items. When you leave the plastic covering on, you are trapping the chemicals onto the garment. In addition, these plastic bags take up a lot of room in the closet and make seeing your wardrobe really challenging.

Note: I get a lot of push back here.

"I keep my clothes in the plastic bags to protect from dust." If you have that much dust in your closet, you have another problem to solve. If you are using longer-term storage, purchase a few garment storage bags for these items.

"If an item is in the plastic bag, I know it's clean and ready to be worn." If it's in your closet, it should be clean and ready to be worn. Clothes that need to be laundered before being worn again do not belong in your closet; they are cluttering up your wardrobe. Creating an effective rotation of the items in your closet is important and vital to making your wardrobe work for you.

Try sectioning off a space for recently worn items. Some clients change the direction of the hanger to indicate an item was worn recently. Be creative to figure out what will work for you without taking up valuable space within your closet.

Be intentional about how you store your clothes and create zones. Do not skip this step! Again, clients often want to just shove everything back into the closet and be done with the project. As an organizing coach, I walk them through how they use their wardrobe. If you need work clothes 70 percent of the time, why are party clothes front and center? Use the best real estate for your most common items. For some, putting like items together is most helpful. All the long sleeves go together and then short sleeve tops. Bottoms in another section segmented by work or non-work. Depending on your work environment, there might be a lot of cross-over in your wardrobe, so play with your closet organization and see what works best for you. Some clients put like colors together for easy reference within the different categories.

To maximize hanging space, install metal butler hooks or removable command hooks inside the closet and on the doors. These work great for a multitude of items including hooded sweatshirts, belts, pajamas, and accessories. By using this space, you've immediately found more room within your closet. Go back and review Chapter 10: Maximizing My Space to find some hidden and bonus storage areas. If you're really space challenged, get creative. In my son's first post-grad apartment, he had really limited space and a pretty extensive wardrobe including his professional clothes. His bedroom closet was small and narrow and not conducive to hanging dress shirts and pants. We took the door off of his closet and put open racking in for his folded items. In his entryway landing, we used a freestanding portable wardrobe for all his professional, hanging clothes. And command hooks. Lots of command hooks.

Once you've tackled the closet, start on the drawer and any cabinet space. Simple rack systems from home improvement stores are great stand-ins for traditional bureaus and come at a great price point. Or if you prefer the look and option of closed storage, check out your local furniture consignment shop for a gently used bureau. With drawers and cabinets, the process is the same. Remove everything and create categories: donate, try on, and Not Today. Welcome to the land of a million T-shirts! How do we possibly accumulate so many T-shirts? This is a great opportunity to remove the T-shirts that are really memorabilia and not an actual part of your wardrobe. Thinning out this way will make a big difference. Think about saving or displaying your favorite T-shirts as memorabilia either in a shadow box or T-shirt quilt. Take another read through Chapter 22: Honoring Your Legacy for ideas.

This is an opportunity to create space and ease in your life— embrace it! Purge the stained T-shirts. Move on the shorts and pants that don't fit. Get rid of the mismatched socks, stretched out pajama pants and tragic underwear. How many pairs of white athletic socks does one person need? Unless you have limited access to a washer and dryer, fewer is better. Your college days are (likely) over. You deserve better.

After you pare down what you have, you can determine where items are best stored. Go back and revisit your wardrobe planning. Give your often-worn items top priority in your drawers. Segment your clothes by use: nightclothes, socks and underwear, workout gear, casual tops and bottoms. Figure out your unique system and work from there. There is no right or wrong way to manage this project; it should be intuitive to you. I keep my sweaters and my husband's heavy sweatshirts in an armoire in my guest room. We don't have room in our bedroom closet to store these items so they work best in another space.

Now that you've tackled your clothing repeat this process with your accessories. Organize your shoes, scarves, bags, and belts. I am neither a shoe person nor a bag person, but I know many! I have seen shoe and bag collections worthy of Imelda Marcos. We all should have special occasion bags and shoes; yes, even the men. How many shoes and bags you keep is entirely up to you. What is critical is that the items you keep are ones you actually use. In the case of shoes especially, be sure any pairs you keep are in good shape. It does not matter how expensive your shoes are if they are in poor condition. Find a cobbler and have them resoled if that makes sense so that they have true value by being worn. Shoes sitting unworn and unused in your closet are a waste of money, space, and use.

So, let's talk about wasting money, space, and use. I've seen a lot of client frustration around wasted money on purchases that just aren't being used. And that's a normal reaction. But here's the thing … holding onto that frustration and that thing only increases the negativity. "Don't throw good money after bad," as my mother would say. Cut your losses and walk away from something you are not wearing or using. The tax donation may be enough as well as knowing that you've made a positive difference. This may be enough to make the letting go easier. But what if your item has real value?

In Chapter 8: What Do I Do with All This Stuff? I spent a lot of time talking about intrinsic value versus perceived value. When we're talking about donating a lot of clothes and accessories, this is a question that clients often ask. The last few years have seen huge growth in the online resale market both for designer as well as mass retailers. There are specialty sites that deal with only very high-end designers and products—TheRealReal and Rebagg are just two examples. You can sell most clothes on eBay or Facebook Marketplace; each has value if you want to recoup some of your initial cost. Clients also consign higher end items at consignment shops, which are definitely making a resurgence. Reselling, consigning, and donating your unneeded and unused items gives them new life—reduce, reuse, recycle—and might bring you some cash as well. The real value, however, lies in opening up that space in your closet and drawers, not for more stuff, but to wear and enjoy what you already have.

Iris Apfel, the American businesswoman, interior designer, and fashion icon put it this way: "Fashion you can buy, but style you possess." You bring forth your style and authenticity by the way you choose to live in congruence with your true values, not just through the clothes you wear.

Closets and drawers can be challenging spaces. Clothes can be much more than just things you wear. They can be memories of special times and events. These items can represent motivation and sometimes disappointment. Working with an organizing professional can help you break through your roadblocks; keep what you love and get rid of the rest.

26

Safety First

*"Civilization rests on the fact that most
people do the right thing most of the time."*

—Dean Koontz

uick, name the one space in your home that is really disorganized and in need of some serious decluttering. Many clients say basement, playroom, or closets. Yes, these are often trouble spots in the home. But one of the most important spaces that often gets overlooked is the medicine cabinet/bathroom storage. For many of us, it's a space we use multiple times a day, but we rarely give it a thought unless we need something specific. On a daily basis, we rummage around for the item we need and then shove everything back in and close the door. In theory, we know that there's a lot of "stuff" lurking in there that we should address and yet we rarely focus on it. Things can literally "get lost" in the jumble and we don't take the time to sort it out. While a medicine cabinet may seem like a low organizing priority, I urge you to rethink that. This kind of space needs to be prioritized both for ease of use and most importantly, for safety.

Here's the simple truth: We all lose and misplace things sometimes and for some of us, the frequency is greater. Try this prayer to Saint Anthony if you find yourself in that situation—it certainly can't hurt! "Saint Anthony, who received from God the special power of restoring lost things, grant that I may find (insert your missing item here) which has been lost." And while prayer is great, better organization can be even more impactful.

What happens when a medical situation arises and we can't find the first aid or health items we need? Do you want to be explaining to your hurt child or partner that you just know that medicine he needs is in here somewhere, hidden behind half-empty and expired products?

This book isn't a guide to a "perfectly organized" space. It's a framework for living in an intentional way so that you can live your best life. So, yes, safety first. In our overfilled and overscheduled lives, we often careen from one moment to the next and don't stop and take the time to be mindful of what keeps us safe and living our best life. Are you making mindful choices in what you purchase and bring into your space? Are you making intentional decisions about what you eat and how you move your body? Do you take the time to review your legal and financial matters so that you and your loved ones are prepared and protected? Being organized isn't about your stuff; it's about how you live your life.

Slow down and be safe.

I have a very good friend who works as a risk auditor for an insurance company. His job is to assess how safe buildings and structures are to mitigate risk to the insurer. Why he is so good at his job? Because he is intentional and questions "the why" in every scenario. In every decision he makes, both personal and professional, he is intentional in his decisions and actions; it has even earned him the nickname "Safety Dave." He is in excellent health and is in a very solid financial position because he always considers the risks and rewards in any given situation. Dave will choose kale over Oreos (most of the time!) because he recognizes that the short-term high of eating an Oreo does not outweigh the long-term benefits of eating the kale. He addresses what needs to happen in the now to be able to enjoy the benefits of that action in the future. Much of organizing is like that. Doing the "hard stuff" today to reap the benefits; with less stress and more space, time, and joy in your life.

Did you know that pharmaceuticals should not be stored in a bathroom medicine cabinet? Yup, that was news to me as well.

Organizing Tip

The first thing to address in a medicine cabinet is expiration dates. Dates are there for a reason so always err on the side of caution. Unfortunately, there is no industry standard as to where the expiration dates appear. These dates are sometimes on the packaging, other times stamped on the tops or bottoms of bottles. Get out your glasses! Anything that is three months past its expiration date should be discarded.

Most medicine should be stored at room temperature and kept away from heat and moisture. Because any bathroom with a shower is prone to high temperatures and humidity, it is a poor place to keep medication. Heat and moisture break down the components faster so that the drug may lose its effectiveness. In addition, those conditions can cause its chemistry to change so there is a danger that the medication could become harmful. Ideally, store OTC medications in a kitchen cabinet or hall closet.

> **Caveat:** All prescription medication should be kept in a locked space—not in the easy access of a medicine cabinet. We all need to take responsibility for the proper use and storage of these medications. The first place a burglar is going to look in your home is the medicine cabinet for any opioids. I know firsthand people who have had pain medications stolen from their home by guests and service providers; be proactive and responsible about this.

Put aside any medications that have expired. Do not flush these down the toilet! These chemicals seep into the ground and drinking water and can cause real harm. Yes, I know that the old recommendation was to flush any unused medication but the recommendations have changed. Any prescription medications should be disposed of properly. The US Drug Enforcement Agency (DEA) conducts biyearly Drug Take Back Days in many communities. You can find a local drop off spot and more information at https://www.deadiversion.usdoj.gov/drug_disposal/takeback/. At the April 2018 National Drug Take Back Day, local law enforcement agencies collected a total weight of 949,046 lbs. (474.5 tons) of medication in one day.[14] Check with your local police department to see if they have a drop box for expired prescriptions. If there isn't one in your community, ask and advocate about how to get one.

> **Caveat: Technically, only prescription drugs need to be disposed of in this manner; however, I generally include any OTC medications. I am already making a trip to the drop box so I add these to the pile. Follow the practice that feels right for you.**

My local police department also has a SHARPS box for safe disposal of medical needles. For anyone who has a medical condition for which they use injectable drugs, you know how quickly these needles can pile up. Some drug companies provide a "ship back" program for these items but we must take the time to complete this task. I have helped several clients safely dispose of these items which had been amassed over time. No, this is not a fun task. No, this won't necessarily make your home look more organized but the value of doing this is far greater. Remember the two minute rule of organizing? If a task will take two minutes, stop and do it now. These kinds of tasks warrant taking that time.

Once you've eliminated the unneeded, unused, and expired medications from your medicine cabinet, determine what should be put back in. A bent, half-ripped box of Q-tips is not an ideal storage solution. This is an important spot to choose easy to use storage; you don't generally have a lot of time to get to these items so make your life easier. Containerize like items—such as first-aid items like bandages and oint-

Organizing Tip

This is a space in which I highly recommend decanting products into a different container for more efficient storage. We all have several open, half-used boxes of Band-Aids in our medicine cabinet. Take those out of the box and put them all in a plastic bag with the antibiotic ointment. Voilá, a first aid kit that you can grab from the cabinet when needed. I recommend the same method with fancy "first aid" kits. Yes, the little boxes and bags are cute. Yes, it may even fit inside the medicine cabinet. But can you clearly see inside? Do you really know what you have when you need it? Are there important items that won't fit inside the designated container? You don't have to hold onto the original container—recycle it and move on.

ments—in zip top bags or small acrylic containers. Group like items together—shaving, hair products, dental items—inside the cabinet for easy access.

Do you have duplicates of the same item? Extra unopened bandages and athletic tape? A second bottle of pain reliever? A new unopened bag of cotton balls that falls out every time you open the door? For these items, I use the term "overflow." These are the extras that we will use next; this is a great way to be prepared. However, these items do not need to stay in with your everyday items. Store the unopened items in another spot to leave the prime real estate of the medicine cabinet free.

Repeat this process with each category: makeup, shaving, oral care. A few years ago I bought all the men in my family the same razor system. Now I only have to buy one brand of razor blades instead of trying to figure out what goes with which handle. Honestly, don't I have better things to do than stand in front of the shaving section and try to figure this out? Yes. I have lots of better things to do so I simplified the process and my life.

Remember all the work you did setting up your landing/launching pad? Now it's time to talk about the items that should be housed here that will keep you and your family safe. How about sunscreen and bug spray?

Today we're better educated about the damage that can result from overexposure to the sun and the risk of mosquito- and tick-borne illnesses. The occurrence of melanoma has been increasing for decades and Eastern Equine Encephalitis and especially Lyme disease diagnoses have exploded in recent years. A recent CDC report has noted that since the

Organizing Tip

If your bathroom space is really limited or there are a number of family members sharing this space, consider using a shower caddy. These handled caddies get a lot of use in dorm settings but when my boys are home from their apartments, they still use them at home. This allows them to keep their toiletry items in their rooms so again no wondering whose is whose stuff. For those with a lot of products, these caddies are a great solution. Girls love them for makeup, hair, beauty products, and styling tools.

late 1990s, the number of reported cases of Lyme disease in the United States has tripled.[15] And the research into the long-term effects of Lyme is very disturbing.

To make it easier to use proper protection, house your sunscreen and bug spray in your transitional space if possible. If you can see these items in your "exit" space, it's easier to remember to use them before heading outside. Containerize the products into a basket or bin that is safely away from small hands. Be sure to include any furry family members' safety products here as well. Dogs are especially vulnerable to tick transmitted illnesses. Your veterinarian can recommend sprays, collars, and spot-on topical products that kill and repel ticks. As always, make sure these products are stored out of reach of young children, and store these items out of direct sunlight to maintain and extend their product lifespan.

Sun and skin safety are critical to our health and wellness. We use these items before going outside so keeping them

Organizing Tip

Sunscreen should be applied thirty minutes prior to being in the sun—so waiting until you are standing on the beach to apply it is not ideal. I also keep sunscreen and bug spray in my car so that I always have them. This is one area that I recommend a lot of duplication around. The American Academy of Dermatology recommends that when outdoors, reapply sunscreen approximately every two hours so having backups in the car or diaper bag is ideal. As always, check the expiration dates on these products every season.

in the transitional space will make using them at the top of our minds. Safety is one of the primary considerations when talking about organizing. Yes, we want aesthetics, but all our spaces should primarily serve our needs, and safety is one of the biggest. Am I safe now?

If you are regularly clearing out your medicine cabinet and using sunscreen and bug spray, you are making clear, intentional choices about your health and well-being. So what other "safety" choices can you focus on? Are the batteries in the smoke detector and carbon monoxide detector in good working order? Are there spaces that need new light bulbs or more lighting? Do these questions seem silly? You'd be surprised. In working with clients, I have seen disconnected and broken detectors in need of a simple battery change and dark rooms and corners without a working light bulb.

A real organizing, and life, priority is ensuring your health and safety. Stop and find the batteries for the smoke detector. Do you not have a working smoke detector and carbon monoxide detector? Here's the two-minute rule in all its glory: Get on your device, go to Amazon and order it now. Right now. There is no higher priority than being safe in your home. Is finding a battery that fits a challenge? Thankfully the days of needing a 9-volt battery are over; most detectors take AA batteries now. Do you need a battery for the detector? Again, Amazon Prime at your service. If you are not an online shopper—and I know you exist because I've worked with you—write it down on your to-do list and get it done today. The text to your girlfriend, the next episode of *Game of Thrones*, or the playoff game is not more important than moving forward with anything related to your safety. No excuses on this one.

Organizing Tip

The key to living an organized and intentional life is being adaptive. When I work with clients, the systems we create are adaptive to the space and the present needs. So while we focus on how to make the situation better in the near term, we keep open options for the future. Your children will not always be toddlers trying to open the cabinets under the kitchen sink. Before you know it, they will be heading off to high school. So it's safe to take off those cabinet locks which are just getting in your way.

While we're here, let's talk about that dank space under the sink. When was the last time you excavated everything from under the sink and really knew what you had under there? Ummm, never? That open space under the sink, kitchen, and bathroom, is a catch-all, mostly because it's open space. Some clients create extra space by adding a wire shelf, which is a great option. To maximize that space and make corralling and using your cleaning products easier, I recommend using a cleaning caddy with a handle. Again, this goes back to the advantage of portability like using these for toiletry items in and out of the bathroom. I put all my cleaning products in the caddy and pull it out for easy access. The caddy can be carried from room to room and floor to floor. This eliminates bottles and cans strewn all over the bottom of the cabinet and takes better advantage of the vertical space. I also have a separate, smaller caddy for my ironing supplies. I take out the entire caddy with the linen spray, spray starch, lint roller, and water bottle for the iron and bring it into the room I am ironing in (either the kitchen or living room). My mother spent hours ironing; I spend minutes. I like to think she would approve of my ironing caddy if not my technique.

It goes without saying that the cleaning products under your sink are very harmful to humans and pets alike. Be sure cabinets storing chemicals are fully secured if you have pets or children in the home. There are even companies that will come and baby-proof your home with locks and gates. Genius! Proper disposal of cleaning and laundry products is critical. Check out if your town has a hazardous waste collection day or is part of a regional cooperative. This is an opportunity to safely dispose of these powerful chemicals in a safe and timely manner. If you have open chemical items, gather them up and store them securely out of the way until you can dispose of them safely. Yes, you can throw them in the trash if your recycling allows that but again, pouring these down the drain is not ideal. Decide what your comfort level is with this process and get it done. This is not a place to skimp on safety.

Sometimes we throw up roadblocks to our own success because we don't adapt our systems to changing situations. In these instances, sometimes the simplest changes have a great impact. I had a client who was still using a baby gate to keep her child out of the laundry room because of the chemicals stored in there. This was a great system for when the child was a toddler and needed to be kept out of the space. Every time the parents wanted to get into the room, which was often because it housed other items as well, they had to climb over the gate. And their daughter was six. They had created a system that was necessary and helpful at the time. But as their needs changed, they failed to adapt and change with that so they literally created an unnecessary, physical roadblock for themselves. What are your roadblocks? Do you need to add (or remove) cabinet locks or baby gates? Did you create a system that was effective years ago but now makes your life harder instead of easier? Don't make things harder than they have to be; this only creates more stress and complexity in your space. Your home should be a place that rejuvenates you and brings you joy and keeps you safe.

CHAPTER

27

It's Not about the Stuff

"Pleasure is an attempt to fill yourself.
Joy is what you are."

—**Byron Katie**

ebster's Dictionary defines joy as, "the emotion evoked by well-being, success, or good fortune." When was the last time you remember being joyful? Honest to goodness, feeling tearfully, deeply, joyful? I'm guessing that moment was not about your stuff. Purchasing things can give us a temporary pleasure, a "high" of having something new and shiny. Unfortunately, this is often followed by a crash of sadness and regret when we realize we overspent and this "thing" doesn't really make us happy. So we keep buying more and more to get back to that "high" and the negative cycle continues. But joy cannot be bought; it comes from inside and creates our legacy. Our legacy is how we are defined and remembered. How do you want to be remembered? As the saying goes, "When you die, no one will stand up at your funeral and say, 'She had a really expensive couch and great shoes.'" Don't make your life about stuff.

I have worked in all manner of spaces: Homes that are 1,400-square feet to 7,600-square feet. From small, one-person offices to giant warehouses. It doesn't matter how much space you have; if you buy into a scarcity mentality that life is hard and things might disappear some day, you will fill that space. We buy and buy and overconsume, "buying" into the consumer mentality that our happiness and joy is just that next purchase away. The scarcity mindset runs on fear. Fear that we won't get what we need and fear that we'll lose what we have. So, we hold onto things more tightly. We are unable or unwilling to see the abundance all around us and believe that what we need in life will be there when we need it. Some of this comes from our belief systems—the way in which we were raised and socialized. And much of it comes from our consumer-obsessed culture that tells us that we can just buy the happiness and joy that we seek.

Attempting to purchase our joy and happiness goes hand-in-hand with believing that because something brings us comfort, then that must be true for others as well. This is a very tricky space to be in. This kind of thinking leads to a hoarding mentality in which we use things to isolate and insulate ourselves. A common cause of this mentality is the stress and overwhelm that fills our lives. We try to keep that stress at bay by insulating ourselves with our stuff. The rising volume of clutter serves both as a distraction and an insulator to the issues and challenges we just don't want to face. Much like other ways of numbing ourselves and our lives, the clutter and the hoard keep us so busy, we don't have time to recognize and focus on our true priorities.

Amassing a volume of stuff has many negative causes, not the least of which is an inability to make effective and intentional decisions about our things and our space. If we sit in the scarcity mindset, the results are generally negative, not only to ourselves but to others in our lives. Not only is the clutter overwhelming to us personally, we often end up burdening others with our stuff. I have seen some very negative dynamics within families and organizations due to this. This mindset is not uncommon in senior populations who seek to save, to gift, to pass on, to "share" much of what they have accumulated in life. A scarcity mindset of fear and lack, often stemming from childhood, results in a tightening grip and an inability to let go. The reasoning is often "I've worked so hard for this and it means so much to me, doesn't it mean the same to my son/daughter/extended family?" Often, it doesn't. These unmet expectations about our stuff can lead to very difficult situations. Our culture and society has changed dramatically in the last few decades, and the possessions valued just a decade or two ago no longer hold sway.

As one of the most mobile countries in the world, Americans are known for their seemingly constant relocations, which is a dramatic shift from prior generations. According to the 2013 U.S. Census, Americans move an average of eleven times in their lifetime and younger people are likely to move more frequently.[16] In this economy, workers need to be flexible and job relocations are the norm. The average job position is about five years, likely necessitating multiple moves over a lifetime. In addition, other factors like marriage, retirement, upsizing and downsizing for family reasons lead to many changes. Is it any wonder then that your son or daughter doesn't want or need your twelve-piece dining room set? Sunday dinners are a Rockwell-themed thing of the past, so the china and silver once so valued have become more of a burden, another unneeded and unused thing to pack and move. And still families hold onto this stuff with the expectation that this will change and it will be needed someday. The past is a really convenient dumping ground for unmet expectations. What is this really about? Do you seek for your family to need and want your stuff or you?

I had a smart, engaged senior client who struggled with letting go of her things. Even after downsizing into a significantly smaller space, she remained unwilling to let go of many items that she no longer had space for. After offering all of this to her children multiple times, the items remained, unneeded and unwanted. Not because they didn't love her or appreciate her beautiful things. It was because that was not their lives. They had their own stuff and did not have the space to use and honor their mother's things. In situations like this, this stuff becomes a burden, not just for you but for those you seek to gift or leave these items to.

In each moment and with every decision, we have an opportunity to make a choice. I can intentionally decide that I just don't need another pair of shoes or another purse or a newer phone. That's an intentional decision and I am responsible for the outcome. Conversely, I can choose to be an avid consumer and fill my life with stuff. In either case, I get to decide for myself. It's an opportunity for me to control my life and my outcomes and not leave those important decisions to others.

It's when we defer those decisions and push them out onto others that we lose that control. Working on that downsizing project with my senior client was challenging, but my mantra remained consistent: "Today you get to decide what happens with your things. If you choose not to make that decision, someone else will decide. And know that the decision others will make for your beloved things will likely be different." Decide to decide. Today. Your legacy is not about your stuff.

Have you ever wondered why you can't get or stay organized? Do you think it's about the stuff you have? Honestly, it's rarely about the stuff; it's about why and how we keep our stuff that bogs us down. You are responsible for what enters your space. If you can stem the flow of items into your space, organizing what you already have becomes easier because it cuts down on the volume. So, if struggling to get organized isn't just about the stuff, then what is it about? Are you buying more stuff out of sadness, boredom, guilt, or another feeling? Stuff should serve our needs; we shouldn't be serving our stuff. There is already so much that we have in our space that is physical clutter. Have you stopped to think about the mental clutter you are "consuming"?

In his excellent book, *The Charge: Activating the 10 Human Drives that Make You Feel Alive,* Brendon Burchard talks about the burden of data and information that fills our lives and our spaces. All of this information is literally creating new neural pathways in our brains and changing our ability to process and manage data. "For every bit of data that comes into your life, your brain attaches meaning and emotion to it. It means that information is actually quite 'heavy,' and the more information coming into your life, the more weight is loading you down."[17] How can you be joyful and in the moment when you are weighted down with all this physical and mental stuff? The answer is: you're not. When you are unhappy and dissatisfied, you use negative habits to feed your need for consumption and distraction.

Is shopping a way to pass the time or feel "better"? We even have a name for it: retail therapy! Sure, this is fine once in a while. But if shopping and overconsuming (of food, alcohol, social media, and other habits) are your main outlets for "pleasure," you are missing out on finding the joy in life. As a culture, we spend billions every year to keep death at bay and desperately seek the next fountain of youth. Death isn't the worst thing that can happen to us; in the present, a detachment from living is. We've become very good at avoiding dealing with challenges in the short-term by distracting ourselves and insulating ourselves with our stuff. In the end, it's that avoidance that leads to suffering when we realize that we have squandered so much time and so much money on things that don't really matter at all. We put a higher priority on the trappings of success and having all the biggest and newest toys; we've bought into someone else's version of success.

If recreational shopping is a consistent activity or hobby, change the pattern. Find a new hobby or other activity that will serve you better like spending time with friends (not while shopping!) or working on a creative project. Create a challenge for yourself—no shopping for anything but true necessities for thirty days. See how much money, time, and energy you save. Use up all the "extra" and "overflows" in your home that you've stockpiled and open up that space. Yes, we think we're saving money when we buy bargains or in bulk, but the reality is that these things are taking up time and space that might be put to better use. One of the most frequent phrases I hear from clients is: "I forgot I bought that!" If *that* is something without an expiration date, use it now. Unfortunately, you're not saving any money in the long run when you have to throw out expired products. Your money and time has a greater purpose than standing in line at Target or shopping online at midnight. Your time is better spent reading, engaging with others, learning, and being more connected.

The motivational speaker Jim Rohn famously said that we are the average of the five people we spend the most time with. When it comes to relationships, we are greatly influenced by those closest to us. Your brain is biologically built to mimic what you see and feel in others; scientists call this learned behavior "emotional contagion." This affects our way of thinking, our self-esteem, and our decisions. So the neurons fire over and over and the pattern and habits of consumption repeat. Trying to "keep up with the Joneses" and finding our worth, pleasure, and value in what we have versus what we are leads us to need to continue to consume to keep up.

In the same way over-shopping and over-consuming is a negative pattern, disorganization is a habit that needs to be rewired. With organization, it's not about the how; it's about the why. I can work with a client to create the most effective organizing system possible, but if the habit of maintaining it isn't there, it will be ineffective. When a habit emerges, the brain stops fully participating in decision-making. Unless you deliberately fight a habit, or create a new routine or system, that old pattern will unfold automatically. Unfortunately, as smart and evolved as we are, our brains can't tell the difference between a bad habit and a good habit. You can call this backsliding, yo-yo dieting, or whatever you wish. That's why we have to actively work at our new, organized routines and habits because the old habits are lurking back there, waiting to return.

Tony Dungy, Superbowl-winning coach of the Indianapolis Colts, spent years teaching his teams the power of habit and routines. He saw the value of creating ingrained habits that his players literally didn't have to think about to be successful. "Champions don't do extraordinary things. They do ordinary things, but they do them without thinking, too fast for the other team to react. They follow the habits they've learned." Work with an organizing professional to create intuitive, adaptive systems that meet your intended goals. Be open to changing habits and routines that will support you and your organizing systems. This is where coaching and motivation are key to keeping you on track. Like working with a personal trainer, financial advisor or nutritionist, choose a professional to guide you, provide structure and accountability, and then go, live your best life.

28

Wellness and Wholeness

"Whatever you can do or dream you can do, begin it. Boldness has genius, power, and magic in it."

—John Anster, inspired by Goethe's *Faust*

In 2015, I did a 180 degree shift on my eating and fitness and over a year, let go of fifty pounds. And I've kept if off. At 51, I feel better than I ever have in my life. But that doesn't mean that it was easy. Or that I don't have to be consistently attentive to maintaining my fitness. This isn't something that I sort of pay attention to, every once in a while. It is ongoing, intentional behavior and a mindset—day in, day out. That doesn't make it difficult; it makes it mindful. Getting organized and staying organized is the same. You have to work through the hard stuff to "lose" what's weighing you down and then be mindful about not "putting it back."

Clients sometimes come to me after living with disorgani-zation, stress, and clutter for years. They have struggled to get caught up and get ahead, often to no avail. Some have worked with other organizers and while initially the results were positive, the long-term change never happened. Other clients have read many organizing books and shared the insights with me—all of which were great. And again, the "tips and techniques" outlined in the books were definitely helpful, but not significant enough to disrupt and replace the habits and patterns of disorganization. Frustration, disappointment, and stress resulted. Why couldn't these new "techniques" make lasting change?

Here, I digress and share my personal "aha" moments that led me to lasting change. And thank you, Oprah, not only for this wonderful phrase, but for your authenticity and gratitude that I desire to emulate on a daily basis. This is especially important for me as it was this desire to live my best life through two specific "aha" moments that have led me here today. The first was back in February 2010 at my annual Girls Weekend with my girlfriends. Started in earnest in 1999, we've had over twenty years of weekends that are some of the most consistent touchstones in my life. This weekend has a history of raucous laughter, inside jokes, tear-filled conversations, and moments of utter clarity and vulnerability that are some of the best moments of my life. I had just finished my O Magazine article on "Live Your Best Life"—thank you again, Oprah. I was talking with my girlfriends about my desire to leave my unfulfilling work as a recruiter and do something I loved and was passionate about—being a professional organizer. I was overwhelmed by the idea of leaving my predictable and comfortable position and starting my own business, from scratch, with no business model. In essence, the "hows" of starting were my stumbling block. After feeling angsty and basically whining about how dissatisfied I was with my present work and why I wanted to start on this journey, I'm sure my girlfriends were quite sick of listening to me. With utter simplicity and clarity, my friend Sue looked at me and said, "So, do it." Two months later, I quit my job and started my business.

That simple belief, that I could *be* and *do* what my heart and soul truly desired, set me on the path to the most amazing job I could ever dream of. I have worked with some of the most amazing, kind, generous, intelligent, and supportive clients anyone could ever imagine working with. I have been supported by other organizers and an amazing industry organization, The National Association of Productivity & Organizing Professionals (www.napo.net), which works to educate, inform, and elevate this much-needed industry. I have been mentored and coached by seasoned entrepreneurs who gladly shared their experience and expertise so that we might all succeed and grow. "All boats rise in the tide." I have partnered with other professionals in a desire to share knowledge and resources with our clients in a community of sharing and support. It is because of all this that I am able to share this book with you, so that you might find some guideposts along your journey to living your best life. Because we all deserve to live our best lives.

My second "aha" moment was just as significant and unfortunately, took another five years to arrive. In September 2015, I returned home after visiting my older son who was studying abroad in New Zealand. While I was away, my younger son had left for a post-grad year and after twenty years my house was empty of children. I vividly remember standing in my kitchen, feeling completely and utterly overwhelmed by the enormity of it all and realizing, "This. This is the rest of my life." I knew, in that moment, that I could choose to continue to live as I had been for forty-eight years, and I would end up with my default life. Overweight, pain in my knees and back, unable to do any sort of cardio … and that was my future. In that moment, I decided that I wanted different. And better. I finally fully recognized that I deserved better; that I deserved to live my best life. I started an eating and fitness regimen that week and never looked back.

So … why am I sharing my professional and wellness journey in a book about organizing? What does one have to do with the other? Actually, it has a lot to do with the habits that drive our behavior. In his excellent book, *The Power of Habit*, Charles Duhigg explains how habits, both good and bad, develop. "Habits emerge because the brain is constantly looking for ways to save effort." In fact, Duhigg found that 40 percent of the actions we perform every day aren't decisions; they're habits. When we develop positive keystone habits (being organized, focusing on our wellness, being mindful of our actions and decisions), it starts a process that over time transforms and overrides other habits and creates a chain reaction of positivity in our lives. "The habits that matter most are the ones that, when they start to shift, dislodge and remake other patterns."[18] What we are creating then is synergy; when the whole is greater than the sum of the parts.

Maya Angelou said it best, "Now that I know better, I do

Organizing Tip

Educate yourself on the many options available for eating and fitness plans. Find a trusted coach or professional to help you on this journey. There are so many good programs out there; find the one that fits your life and personality. All programs can be successful; the key is to find the one that will be successful for you. And don't give up if the first one isn't the right fit or you don't see immediate results. Keep working at it because you deserve it.

better." When I learned about organizing as a profession and apprenticed with established organizers, I could create my own model of success. When I had a better understanding of nutrition and exercise, I got fitter and healthier. In order to accomplish that, I had to create an environment that supported my new, healthier habits. I created dedicated workout space in my basement and quit my (underused) gym membership. I could come up with twenty excuses not to go to the gym but I could come up with zero excuses not to walk down the stairs to my basement and workout for thirty minutes. I started getting up earlier in the morning so I would have no excuse not to get a workout in. I revamped my eating. I didn't make one salad, I made four. I prepped vegetables in bulk and cooked large servings of healthy carbs to eat during the week. I organized my life so that I could support my new habits. Because my *why*, my desire for a healthier and fitter life, drove me to keep up with my new habits. Being fit isn't about how I look. It isn't about the numbers on the scale or the tag in my clothes. It's about how I feel and choose to be in this life.

For me, I know that my unhealthy eating was a direct result of not valuing myself and being intentional about my eating. I did not educate myself or find an eating and fitness plan that would benefit me. For a number of my clients, weight and health challenges were accompanied by organizing and clutter challenges.

Much of the overeating and poor nutrition in our culture is a result of the stressful and chaotic lives that we live. With our many responsibilities and frenetic lifestyles, good eating and fitness can fall to the bottom of our priority list. This "time clutter" can lead to poor eating and overconsumption of empty calories. In a cluttered kitchen, the inclination and ability to make healthy meals is significantly diminished. A 2016 study cited by NPR noted that clutter and disorganization can lead to unhealthy eating habits.[19] Clutter can represent loss of control that is echoed back in poor eating habits. Disorganization in the kitchen can be especially problematic as it can promote grabbing junk food or convenience food when stress levels rise. If the kitchen and other areas of the house are causing stress and overwhelm, it's more difficult to make good, healthy food choices.

Here are some tips on organizing your kitchen for better eating:

1. Put away gadgets you don't use. If looking at the expensive appliances you spent "good money" on and aren't using stresses or upsets you, put them away. Store them in high cabinets or in alternate space. Or donate them.

2. Use the prime real estate for the items you use every day. The only appliances that live on my counter are my coffeemaker and my Ninja blender. Both get used multiple times a day so I keep them out.

3. Invest in your wellness. Get the highest quality blender/food processor you can afford. This is an investment in you. If wrestling with a subpar blender or food processor leaves you disinclined to make a healthy smoothie or prepare ingredients, you are shortchanging yourself.

4. Plastic containers make your healthy eating portable. While heating food in plastics is not recommended, these containers are perfect for bringing a salad and veggie snacks to work. I have an abundance of quality plastic containers in various sizes for salads and prepped snacks. I never leave the house without a healthy snack and these containers make it easy.

5. Splurge on a set of quality plastic containers. If you are spending five minutes trying to find a lid to match your container, you are wasting time. Recycle the unmatched, stained, and misshapen containers cluttering up your cabinets. Dedicate a space to your plastic and glass containers for easy use.

6. Group like foods together in your cabinets and pantry. Shallow bins and baskets are great for keeping smaller containers of nuts, seeds, and other add-ins together. In my pantry I use small mason jars for these items as I find it keeps them freshest and they're easy to access.

7. Create a section for any health foods you use consistently. Protein powders, supplements, and vitamins can all be grouped together. If it's easy for you to pull together a healthy smoothie or shake on a daily basis, you'll be more inclined to take the time to do it. If you have to rummage through the cabinets and drawers looking for all the ingredients, it won't happen consistently.

8. Decide how much processed food you are going to bring into your kitchen. Limit easy-grab foods like crackers, cookies, and chips as much as possible and keep snack items in one, harder-to-reach area.

9. Plan menus and make sure you have the needed ingredients. Organize your shopping to support your healthier eating.

10. Prep and cook in bulk. If you're making one salad, it takes three extra minutes to make another (and another…). These will keep in the fridge for days so you have a week's worth of lunches at the ready. I prep veggies in bulk the same way so they are ready for the entire week. I brown all my ground turkey when I buy it and freeze it in 1.5 lb. packages. By doing this, I have this healthy protein ready to use at any time.

11. Frozen is your friend. Keep a stash of frozen fruits and vegetables, which have nearly the same nutritional value as fresh. In a pinch, you can create a delicious, healthy smoothie instead of reaching for ice cream.

Your wellness and wholeness should be one of your highest priorities. Many of us, especially women, put everyone else's needs above our own. We take care of everyone else's needs but often fail to focus on ourselves. We put off getting healthier and eating better and tell ourselves that someday, we'll get to that. Robin Sharma pronounced, "If you don't make time for exercise, you'll probably have to make time for illness." We stay in jobs we don't like, that in some cases are making us ill with stress and unhappiness, because we are afraid of making the change. But in the end, what are we modeling for others in our lives? That we're not important? That taking the time to be healthy and fit isn't a priority? That we have to work at a job we don't like for the money? That life sucks and then you die? Is that what you want to teach your children? Is that how you want to live?

When we stop focusing on the *how*: How to start the business, how to go back to school, how to revamp unhealthy habits, how to declutter a home ... we can get better clarity. We need to focus on the *why*: Why we want to be healthier and live longer, why we want a better education and a new career path, why we want a home that is less cluttered and chaotic. The why is the starting point. "Faith is taking the first step, even when you don't see the whole staircase." The Reverend Martin Luther King gave us that important advice. He did not know all of the hows to make the changes that would become the civil rights movement; he focused on the *why* of justice, love, and equality. Pick your why.

29

Joy in Service

"It is not the style of clothes that one wears, neither the kind of automobile one drives, nor the amount of money one has in the bank that counts. These mean nothing. It is simply service that measures success."

—**George Washington Carver**

When I decided to write this book—or more accurately, *this book decided to write itself*—I intentionally left the section on More Joy until the end. Not because I think more joy is a less worthy goal than more space and more time. The decision really had to do with wanting to share clear, specific techniques to get to more space and more time which are, well, more quantifiable. More joy; that's a bit harder to quantify and recognize. Or is it? Sometimes joy can show up in the most unexpected of places, if only we allow ourselves to see it.

We can all remember times and moments when we felt particularly alive, happy, and joyful. We were keenly aware of being in the moment and connected to others. That's joy. It's these moments that make us profoundly grateful for all that we have. Some folks describe it as being "in the flow" or "clicking on all cylinders" or "getting caught up and losing track of time." Yup, that's joy. It's a quality of knowing and being which often includes others. It is intrinsically tied to feelings of gratitude and it is not uncommon to find those moments in service. When we slow down and take that long look inward, we can acknowledge that the trappings of our lives, the proverbial "frosting on the cake," is just that. It's the outside. It's not what truly makes us happy and joyful. Finding our life's purpose is what brings us joy.

Purpose is a word that can feel very weighted. Webster's defines purpose as "something set up as an object or end to be attained." And our purpose in life can shift and change over time. When we are young, our purpose might be to complete our education and start a career that engages and excites us. This might shift in a few years when we decide to start a family and focus on that, finding our purpose in parenting. At some point, our purpose might change to caring for loved ones who are in ill health or difficult situations. Or maybe our purpose is to create a business. Or write a book. Or become involved with our community, both local and faith based. Or run for political office or the PTO. Finding our purpose is not a luxury reserved for the few; it is essential for everyone.

How many of us find our sense of purpose is through service, to ourselves and others. It was Gandhi who said, "The best way to find yourself is to lose yourself in the service of others." Being in service puts us in the moment, something

Organizing Tip

There are so many ways for you to serve. If you are looking for a volunteer opportunity, spend some time thinking about what you love and what excites you, then tailor your service to meet those needs. Love animals? Volunteer at the local shelter. Are you a knitter or seamstress or quilter? Make and donate items to your local shelter or hospital. Sometimes we serve by simply being there for another, holding the space for grief or sadness. In volunteering and serving, you are limited only by your imagination.

we find in very short supply in our modern culture. Service takes us out of the observer role in our lives and puts us in the warrior role. It is through action that we grow, become, and manifest the life that we truly want to live and as Sheryl Sandberg would say, "Lean in."

It's not only us as individuals that we benefit from serving others; research has shown that businesses and the economy get a significant boost as well. In 2016, *Forbes* magazine reported on the goal of corporations to bring lasting change and growth to the workplace. Despite the significant amount of money spent on employee training and education each year the results were underwhelming. It was the expansion of corporate volunteer programs that was seen as most impactful and well worth the personnel and financial investment. The Harvard Business School study that *Forbes* quoted found that there were four ways a volunteer program produces a high return on investment for a company. Companies that participated and encouraged employee volunteerism saw impacts in improved collaboration, increased self-awareness, impact on revenue, and importance to millennials. Bottom line: When employees see their employer as engaged in more than just "making a buck," they become more engaged in their work. From this, the workplace becomes more positive and the bottom line improves.

For anyone who doesn't work for a large corporation in which these structures already exist, create them. Google "volunteer opportunities" and there's a multitude of resources available to help you structure a program that works. Then act. Sometimes we get stuck in "analysis paralysis" and focus on creating the "perfect program" and then we end up doing nothing. Perfect is the enemy of done. It's hard to go wrong

The Rest Is Just Stuff

The most loving, kind, and generous clients I have worked with over the years embody this sense of purpose and understand the intrinsic role that serving has played in their lives. One client, in addition to having an active, thriving therapy practice, also served as president of her temple. D. understood that serving and giving back to the community that had supported and nurtured her and her family over the years was vital to her purpose in life. One of the healthiest and fittest people I know, she knew the value

(continued)

in serving herself as well. How could she support others if she didn't care and serve herself first? She was always committed to her clients, her family, and her community from a place of wholeness. Working through her beautiful home as we started a decluttering project, her goal was always clear: To continue to live her best life and support others. Moving from room to room, through closets and wardrobes, and space to space, we purged, donated, and cleared out clothes, bedding, accessories, and kitchen items that weren't being used. From rugs to mugs, she let go of anything that was not part of their future and moved it along to those who could use it *today*. We kept what was needed and loved and let go of the rest.

One of the most important goals, which I am thrilled to say we completed together, was to get a handle on all the memorabilia that they had. Both D. and her husband had become the legacy keepers for their families of origin. That meant many, many original photos and documents from each side of the family. In addition, he was an amazing amateur photographer and there were thousands of slides, videos, and photos of their travels, their kids, and their very full lives. When we really started to get our arms around the memorabilia project, I alerted her that the cost would be substantial, potentially thousands of dollars (which is just what it ended up being). Her response? As succinct and to the point as I had come to expect from her: "It's only money; our memories are priceless." Nailed it. D. clearly saw the big picture in life. Family, service, wellness and wholeness, legacy; those are the truly important things in life. The rest is just stuff....

when you are volunteering and serving others. Like with any project, focus on your goal, pick your spot and get started.

Other clients have introduced me to the causes and organizations that they serve and are passionate about. Education and community support for children. Theater. Environmental causes. Animal care. Alumni and civic organizations. Coaching. Faith communities. What's important is not what you are passionate about. What's important is that you take action and commit yourself. Have you ever heard the phrase, "If you want something done, ask the busiest person you know?" For those of us in "helping" professions, our tendency is to, well, *help*. We are doers, and completers, and those Type A personalities. The challenge for us is that we stay focused on serving (being of use) and not assuming responsibility for the outcome. Doing anything is usually better than doing nothing so pick your passion and get moving.

Name the most alive, engaged person you know. Chances are that person is also intentional, active, and in service. Again, this isn't about trying to end world hunger or stop climate change, which are wonderful goals by the way. This is about living a purposeful, intentional life and doing good as part of that. "I don't know what your destiny will be," said Albert Schweitzer, "but one thing I know; the only ones among you who will be really happy are those who will have sought and found how to serve."

30

Getting Started

*"Success is stumbling from failure to failure
with no loss of enthusiasm."*

—Anonymous

We are all on a journey in life; that's the good news. The other good news is that we are in control and responsible for how that journey unfolds. The truth is that you are wholly responsible for how your life is now and how it will turn out. Oh, I can hear the shouting and denials from here!

"You don't understand my life. I've had this happen to me and that happen to me; that's why I can't be successful."

"I don't have enough money/education/training/love/whatever to be happy."

"There's so much going on with my child/partner/boss/company/neighbor/ that I can't make changes now to better my life."

Organizing Tip

If you have unresolved issues with traumatic experiences from your past that keep you from moving forward, find someone who can help. We all need to work through the experiences and situations that we haven't been able to process or integrate into our lives; that's normal. Some folks need a glass of wine and empathetic friends. Some folks need a licensed professional and pharmaceuticals. Neither solution is good or bad; it just is. Stop beating yourself up and staying stuck in your life. Deal with whatever it is that you can't move past so that you can focus on your future. If your vision is a future that's different from your past—organizationally, in your relationships and vocation, with your health—you may need support to get there.

Enough. It's the last chapter. Here's where I'm going to really push back at you: Yes, some really awful, mean, upsetting, and difficult things have happened in your life. These misfortunes, or accidents, or circumstances, or whatever you want to call them have happened. But they do not define you. You are not a victim unless you chose to see yourself as one.

In the end, your perspective is your choice. "It is a rough road that leads to the heights of greatness," stated Seneca. At some point, we all have to decide to make changes. I don't know a friend who hasn't lost a parent, or sibling, or another loved one. We lose jobs, and family, and friends. We have accidents and are in pain. Situations don't turn out like we'd hoped. Our dreams and expectations for ourselves don't materialize and we get frustrated and angry. We blame the government, the economy, the ruling political party, our neighbors, society—pretty much anyone we can in the hope of staving off the reality of who is really responsible. You. You are responsible. We think if we just had a larger salary, or a winning lottery ticket, or "better luck," then everything would be perfect. We'd have what we deserve and all would be right with the world.

This is a victim mindset and a scarcity mentality. It allows you to blame every external situation and circumstance for what's not right in your world. It takes you out of the driver's seat and allows you to create a story about your passivity. "Their life appears to be an industrial slog, ticking off the tasks handed to them by others. They may appear frazzled and frenetic, choking in the tightening clutch of deadlines they did not choose or plan. They often appear to be awaiting instruction and direction, thus their schedule is really more holding pattern than action plan. They get stuck in life because they never rise above their timid desire to please others."[20]

You can't wait around for the life you want to materialize; you have to create your life, one step at a time. Realign your values and thinking and let go of the belief that money and material things will "make" you happy.

Having all the material stuff in the world—all the money, all the trappings and illusions that surround that—does not make you happy or successful. You only have to watch the news to know that many "lucky" people with all those things still self-destruct and live empty, vacuous lives. The rich and famous—who have every advantage you could possibly imagine—disappoint themselves and others consistently. To experience true joy and contentment, you create that from the inside out. Committing to yourself, the people in your life, your work, your passion—that's what creates joy and happiness. The rest is just icing on the cake. We have a responsibility to ourselves and others to use our gifts and abilities to the fullest; anything less is choosing to live less than our best life.

Like anything else in life—work, relationships, health—organization is something that you have to commit to. It does not just appear magically one day and poof, your life is different. Organizing is a process, not an event. I like to quote this old Chinese proverb: "The best time to plant a tree was twenty years ago. The second best time is now." It would be great if we had gotten organized, healthier, more fiscally sound, twenty years ago. That did not happen so let it go. Start today. Hire an organizing coach or professional organizer if getting started is a challenge for you. Start in your most overwhelming space and get going. Know that you can do this. Confidence is a result of taking action; it does not come by thinking about or planning. It comes from doing.

As an organizing coach, I guide my clients to find the best solutions for their specific, individual situations. I do not espouse a "one size fits all" mentality because we're all unique and our situations and organizing challenges are unique. I have helped clients create some truly creative and inspired (and some not-so-inspired) organizing solutions. But that does not mean that like magic, things will always remain organized. We are not always mindful. A crisis or transition comes and we fall off track. We backslide. Stuff happens. We don't stick with our positive habit of putting things back in their appropriate place and clutter starts to build. This is where we need to work to strengthen our new habit of being organized and not allow the clutter and disorganization to spiral downward again. "Our response to any mistake affects the quality of the next moment. It is important to immediately admit and correct our mistakes so that they have no power over that next moment and we are empowered again."[21] In other words, pivot. Pivot away from the old habit and routine of mindlessly allowing items to enter your space and clutter your life. Pivot toward being mindful of everything that enters and dealing with it as it comes in.

This is the intentional start to letting go of clutter and reclaiming your space. And this is the beginning of creating new habits of organization. The winning UCLA basketball coach John Wooden was a fanatic about preparation, repetition, and working on the fundamentals every single day. He understood the value of making the process and habits of practice ingrained in his players. As a result he won ten NCAA national championships in a twelve-year period as head coach at UCLA. "You have to apply yourself every day to becoming a little better. By applying yourself to the task of becoming a little better each and every day over a period of time, you will become a lot better," he said. And it is a practice. Lawyers, doctors, entrepreneurs, technology gurus, artists, salespeople—experts in their field and wildly successful—and yet they still beat themselves up for an inability to get and stay organized. My mother had a wonderful phrase that I use with clients who are struggling, feeling that they should somehow be perfect and be able to do all these things on their own. "God doesn't give with both hands." We all need a little guidance and a coach at some point in our lives.

Decide to decide to get started. Make today the day you start the task of getting better organized. The positive impacts will ripple through your life in many wonderful and sometimes unexpected ways. Be intentional in what you buy and what enters your space. Be mindful of other healthy habits that support your well-being. Don't focus on the "perfect" organization or solution; sometimes good enough really is good enough. Be kind to yourself. Make this journey about learning and growth, not about disappointment and guilt. Create a life and a home that reflects you and the life you want to live. Make the journey about the journey because that's real life.

Take a deep breath. Now, let's go find more space, more time, and more joy!

ABOUT THE AUTHOR

Often asked why she got into organizing, Lisa's answer is always the same—"It's about making your life easier. When my life was especially chaotic and stressful—young children, the demands of growing a business, ill or dying family members, I found that being organized just helped me stay on a more even keel and get through those really tough times. Organization isn't the end goal—happy is the end goal—but being organized goes a long way in making your life easier so that you can focus on the really important things."

Since starting her coaching practice, Lisa has been a member of the National Association of Productivity and Organizing Professionals (www.napo.net), a professional group dedicated to improving our clients' lives, one cluttered space at a time. For almost a decade, Lisa has worked with clients to create organizing systems that work.

Featured in *The Boston Globe* print and online editions, "Professional organizers find steady market for their service," the article highlights some of the work Lisa has done in helping clients find more space, more time, and more joy in their lives. Lisa is a frequent speaker on organizing strategies and project management and has been a guest on local radio stations. In addition, Lisa's work has been featured in local media in articles on organizing tips, along with being included in print and online editions of "30 Ways to Create a Stress-Free Holiday."

A graduate of Boston College, Lisa worked for a number of years in high tech and human resources with extensive experience in hiring and project management. With experience in retail, marketing, and education as well as high tech, Lisa's background allows her to work successfully in a number of settings. Along with volunteer and community work, she is the parent of two adult sons, which makes her an expert in laundry, food preparation, and an avid sports fan. Lisa lives south of Boston with her husband in an organized and joyful home.

ACKNOWLEDGMENTS

More Space. More Time. More Joy! has been a labor of love and a desire to give back in some small measure all that has been paid forward to me.

Figuring out how to best articulate my message was a result of the excellent work of Laura Willis of Encore Revolution. From there, Nancy O'Keefe of Nancy O'Keefe Coaching shared her business coaching and insisted I start to blog. This book is a direct outcome of both of those efforts.

To my publisher Lisa Akoury-Ross and my editor Lisa Schleipfer—you have shepherded me through this sometimes bewildering process in both a professional and loving way—I thank you both.

Every coach needs a coach and I had an exceptional one in Donna Bond of Donna Bond Coaching. It was through my work with Donna that I recognized I needed to share this book with the world. Donna, for your unwavering support and encouragement I reflect back to you the endless light and love you have given me.

To my friends and family, I'm sure you'll see yourselves here—thank you for letting me "practice" on you and thank you for putting up with my mild OCD. A special thank you to Judy, my "handler," and Fran, my "PR and marketing guru"—no girl could ask for better friends and cheerleaders.

To Kevin, Conor, and Brett. For your love, support, and keeping it real for me. And always reminding me when I needed to pick up my own organizational game....

The greatest thank you of all is to my clients. Without your trust in our work together, this book would not exist. Whether we worked together for a day, a month, a year or years, each one of you taught me a valuable lesson. We worked together, we laughed together, and sometimes we cried together—thank you for opening up your homes, your businesses, and your lives to me. Because of our work together, I can share this out with the world so that someone, somewhere, might benefit. I am truly humbled.

Resources

WHERE TO DONATE ANYTHING

One of the biggest challenges to getting organized is what to do with all of the stuff that we no longer want or need. Here is a list of resources in the Boston area that would welcome the donation of your gently used items.

Bridesmaid Dresses and Prom Dresses. Get rid of unwanted tulle at DonateMyDress.org, which distributes prom, Sweet 16, and quinceañera frocks to girls who can't afford them.

Clothing and Household Items: Plenty of organizations will accept your tired attire, but Vietnam Veterans of America resells it to fund programs for veterans and will pick up your donation. Are the items in less than ideal condition? Include it anyway—these are sold by the pound and made into rags.

Construction Material. Contact your local Habitat for Humanity ReStore. ReStores sell donated goods at discounted prices; the money is used to fund the construction of Habitat homes. Each ReStore is different, so contact one in your area for information on what items they take.

Eyeglasses. New Eyes for the Needy sends your old eyeglasses abroad, bringing the gift of sight to places like Bolivia, Ghana, and Cambodia.

iPods. Through Music and Memory, iPods in working condition—as well as donated iTunes gift cards—help lift the spirits of elderly patients with Alzheimer's, multiple sclerosis, and cancer.

Just About Anything. Freecycle, an eight-million-strong "worldwide gifting movement," reduces waste by connecting trash-bound household items—bikes, coffee tables, moving boxes, appliances, birthday party decor, and more—with local people who want them. There's an active group on the South Shore so you know your "gift" will be used locally.

Animal shelters are always in need of these items for their animal clients. Scituate Animal Shelter welcomes these items as well as food and other non-perishables.

Old Cellphones. The phones are sold to a company that recycles them, and Cell Phones for Soldiers uses the money to buy calling cards for troops stationed abroad so they can phone home for free. Go to Cellphones For Soldiers to print a free prepaid shipping label.

Stuffed Animals. Consider donating these furry friends to Loving Hugs, which offers children in war zones, refugee camps, and orphanages a cuddly new friend. Another option is to send them to Stuffed Animals for Emergencies, which donates gently used stuffed animals to homeless shelters, hospitals, and emergency aid workers—paramedics often give the soft toys to kids they meet on their calls.

TechnoTrash. Recycle these items at Best Buy. Drop off your chargers, cords, and technology items—after you've wiped them clean and reset to factory settings.

Toys and Sports Equipment. Big Brother Big Sister Foundation of Massachusetts Bay accepts books and toys, sports equipment, electronics, and most household items and will pick up donations at your location.

Women's Professional Clothing and Accessories. Dress for Success empowers women to achieve economic independence by providing a network of support, professional attire, and the development tools to help women thrive in work and in life. There's a local office on Commonwealth Avenue in Boston.

YOUR WORKING DOCUMENTS

- Bank Statements
- Business Documents
- Credit Card Statements
- Education/School Information
- Health Insurance
- Home Improvement Files
- Insurance: Auto, Property, Umbrella
- Life Insurance
- Mortgage Statements and Paperwork
- Pay Stubs
- Retirement Account Statements
- Utility Bills—Filed Separately: Cable, Electric, Water, Gas
- Volunteer Responsibilities
- Yearly Tax File

YOUR FOREVER
DOCUMENTS

- Adoption Papers
- Automobile Title
- Birth Certificates
- Citizenship Papers
- Copyrights or patents
- Death Certificates
- Divorce Decrees
- Life Insurance Policies
- Marriage Certificates
- Military Discharge Papers
- Passports
- Powers of Attorney
- Property Deeds
- Social Security Cards
- Wills, Trusts, and Estate Plans

ENDNOTES

1. Alexander Harris, "SpareFoot Storage Beat: U.S. self-storage industry statistics," SpareFoot, accessed March 11, 2019, https://www.sparefoot.com/self-storage/news/1432-self-storage-industry-statistics/.

2. Peter Walsh, *It's All Too Much: An Easy Plan for Living a Richer Life with Less Stuff* (New York: Free Press, 2007), 32.

3. "Lost and Found: The Average American Spends 2.5 Days Each Year Looking For Lost Items Collectively Costing U.S. Households $2.7 Billion Annually in Replacement Costs," Cision PRNewswire, (May 2017), https://www.prnewswire.com/news-releases/lost-and-found-the-average-american-spends-25-days-each-year-looking-for-lost-items-collectively-costing-us-households-27-billion-annually-in-replacement-costs-300449305.html.

4. Stephen Covey, *The 7 Habits of Highly Effective People: Restoring the Character Ethic* (New York: Simon and Schuster, 1989), 148–149.

5. "Car Depreciation: How Much Value Will a New Car Lose?," CARFAX, accessed December 2018, https://www.carfax.com/blog/car-depreciation.

6. Stephen Covey, *The 7 Habits of Highly Effective People: Restoring the Character Ethic* (New York: Simon and Schuster, 1989), 158.

7. "Brief diversions vastly improve focus, researchers find," Illinois News Bureau, accessed January 2018, https://news.illinois.edu/view/6367/205427.

8. Sakshi Behl, "13% Employee Productivity Loss due to Social Media in the Workplace," *Digital Vidya* (October 2016), https://www.digitalvidya.com/blog/13-employee-productivity-loss-due-to-social-media-workplace/.

9. "Here's My Habits Manifesto. What's Yours?," Gretchen Rubin, (October 22, 2014), https://gretchenrubin.com/2014/10/heres-my-habits-manifesto-whats-yours/.

10. Lewis Howes, *The School of Greatness: A Real-World Guide to Living Bigger, Loving Deeper, and Leaving a Legacy* (Emmaus: Rodale 2017), 56.

11. Stephen Covey, *The 7 Habits of Highly Effective People: Restoring the Character Ethic* (New York: Simon and Schuster, 1989), 241.

12. Charles Duhigg, *The Power of Habit: Why We Do What We Do in Life and Business* (New York: Random House, 2012), 144.

13. Brendon Burchard, *The Charge: Activating the 10 Human Drives That Make You Feel Alive* (New York: Free Press, 2012), 6.

14. "DEA National RX Takeback," Take Back Day, accessed February, 2019, https://takebackday.dea.gov.

15. "Lyme and other tickborne diseases: Prevention is key in fight against tickborne disease," Centers for Disease Control and Prevention, accessed December, 2018, https://www.cdc.gov/media/dpk/diseases-and-conditions/lyme-disease/index.html.

16. "How Many Times Does the Average Person Move in a Lifetime?," Steinway Moving and Storage, accessed July, 2018, https://www.steinwaymovers.com/news/how-many-times-does-the-average-person-move-in-a-lifetime.

17. Brendon Burchard, *The Charge: Activating the 10 Human Drives That Make You Feel Alive* (New York: Free Press, 2012), 41.

18. Charles Duhigg, *The Power of Habit: Why We Do What We Do in Life and Business* (New York: Random House, 2012), 141.

19. Lenny R. Vartanian, Kristin M. Kernan, Brian Wansink, "Clutter, Chaos, and Overconsumption: The Role of Mind-

Set in Stressful and Chaotic Food Environments," *Environment and Behavior* Vol. 29 Issue 2 (2017): 215–217. https://journals.sagepub.com/doi/abs/10.1177/0013916516628178.

20. Brendon Burchard, *The Motivation Manifesto* (Carlsbad: Hay House, 2014), 112.

21. Stephen Covey, *The 7 Habits of Highly Effective People: Restoring the Character Ethic* (New York: Simon and Schuster, 1989) 91.

More Space. More Time. More Joy!
Organizing Your Best Life
LISA DOOLEY
www.https://yourorganizedlife.biz/

Publisher: SDP Publishing

Also available in ebook format

SDP Publishing

www.SDPPublishing.com
Contact us at: info@SDPPublishing.com

CPSIA information can be obtained
at www.ICGtesting.com
Printed in the USA
LVHW111857181119
637717LV00007B/27/P